Looking Back at Refrigerated Ships

by

Andrew Wiltshire

The **Geestbay** was the first of a pair of modern refrigerated vessels ordered from Smith's Dock Co Ltd of South Bank on Teesside. She was launched on 19 February 1981 and delivered to Geest Industries Ltd, who registered their ships at the Lincolnshire port of Boston. She had a gross tonnage of 7729 and was followed in 1982 by the **Geestport**, both vessels having about 30% greater cargo capacity than the previous Geest ships. She was 521 feet in length and could accommodate twelve passengers in seven cabins. Her four main holds were made up of fourteen cargo spaces, and in addition to hatch access, were served by five side doors on each side of her hull. The **Geestbay** had four electric cranes, two of 8 tons and two of 12.5 tons capacity, and four derricks. She could also carry seventy-two 20' containers of which fifty-two could be housed below deck. Her main engine was a 6-cylinder Burmeister and Wain type of 13100bhp giving her a service speed of 21 knots. Here we see her making a dramatic departure from Barry harbour on 12 June 1991. She was sold in 1994 having been replaced a larger vessel. The **Geestbay** became the **Magellan Reefer** of Aqua Ability SA under the Panamanian flag. After three further name changes, she arrived at Alang, India as the **Estia I** on 22 November 2009, for breaking up.

(Nigel Jones)

INTRODUCTION

The need to transport perishable items by sea has resulted in the development of refrigerated ships. As early as the 1870s, ships were constructed with insulated cargo spaces to facilitate the transportation of meat, dairy products, bananas and other perishable items. For many years elegant refrigerated cargo-liners traded worldwide for companies like Port Line and New Zealand Shipping, but were rendered obsolete by containerisation in the early 1970s. Meanwhile fully-refrigerated ships, later to be refered to as "pure reefers", continued to develop, becoming larger and much more technically advanced in post-war years.

The term "advanced reefer" relates to ships built with separate compartments, each with its own refrigeration plant. These compartments could be maintained at a wide range of temperatures. From the 1980s reefers were then designed so that they could carry cargoes on pallets. The modern reefer is now a sophisticated vessel, incorporating highly sensitive temperature control systems that allow the carriage of delicate perishables in fully automated conditions. Names like Geest, Fyffes, Chiquita, Salen and Lauritzen have long been associated with refrigerated shipping. I personally have many memories of these and others going back to the late 1960s.

This book does not set out to be a definitive work on refrigerated shipping. It is more of a colourful appreciation of the subject in days gone by. For the reader it will hopefully highlight the various types of ship within this category and revive many memories. Some abbreviations used throughout are: grt (gross registered tonnage), bhp (brake horse power), shp (shaft horse power) and TEU (twenty-foot equivalent unit container).

Acknowledgements

This book has been a pleasure to compile over the past few months and has greatly enhanced my knowledge and appreciation of the subject of refrigerated shipping. In addition to my regular supporters, I have made some new and valued acquaintances along the way. My father John Wiltshire has now passed his slide collection to me therefore enabling me to use this as the basis for the book. Nigel Jones and Bob Allen have yet again helped get the project off the ground by making available a large selection of material from their vast slide collections. A big thank you must go out to newcomers Douglas Cromby and Chris Howell for their valued contributions and the time and effort they have willingly given to my requests for help.

As with my earlier books, one of the great inputs has come from my friend Kevin Blair and his contact Paul Hood, who have spent much time chasing up various queries I have raised on individual ships. Thank you for your time and patience. Thanks also to Bernard McCall for his continued support and allowing me to keep this title on the back-burner until the time was right, and to Amadeus who continue to maintain a very high standard of reproduction. Finally I am grateful to my wife Tracey, for allowing me to spend many evenings alone at the computer, putting words to captions, and thumbing through numerous books and records.

Written sources used throughout include copies of *Ocean Ships*, (Ian Allan), various *Lloyds Register* publications, *Merchant Ships World Built*, *Reefer Ships* by Nick Tolerton, *Ships Monthly* magazine and a number of publications on specific shipping companies.

Andrew Wiltshire   Cardiff   September, 2011

Published by Bernard McCall, 400 Nore Road, Portishead, Bristol, BS20 8EZ, England.
Telephone/fax : 01275 846178. E-mail : bernard@coastalshipping.co.uk Website : www.coastalshipping.co.uk
All distribution enquiries should be addressed to the publisher.

Printed by Amadeus Press, Ezra House, West 26 Business Park, Cleckheaton, West Yorkshire, BD19 4TQ.
Telephone : 01274 863210. Fax : 01274 863211. E-mail : info@amadeuspress.co.uk Website : www.amadeuspress.co.uk

ISBN : 978-1-902953-54-0

Front cover: A modern yet handsome vessel, the **Dalmacija Frigo** was a product of the Brodogradiliste "Split" yard in Yugoslavia. She could perhaps be described as the ultimate traditional reefer design to feature derricks as opposed to cranes. Her keel was laid in January 1981, but was not completed until April 1983 for Mediteranska Plovidba. She had a gross tonnage of 10325 and overall length of 496 feet, and was of a conventional layout, with four holds served by four 5-ton derricks and a TEU capacity of 114. Her main engine was a 6-cylinder MAN K6SZ70 of 13460bhp, assembled by Tvornica Dizel Motora "Split" and giving her a speed of 21 knots. From 1991 her home country became Croatia after the break-up of Yugoslavia and the **Dalmacija Frigo** then hoisted the Panamanian flag. By 1998 she was sailing for Frigo Navigation Ltd of Malta and registered in Valletta. We see her here making an impressive sight as she arrives at Marina di Ravenna on 24 September 1998. By 2000 she was working in the Unicool Arctic Reefers pool and in 2003 had her first name change, to **Alma** for Alder Shipping Ltd. In 2006 she became the **Sun Emerald** for Atlantic Trader Navigation of St Vincent and Grenadines, and was sold for breaking up at Alang in May 2010.

(Nigel Jones)

Back cover: The refrigerated cargo liner **Port Caroline** of 16275 grt was the final merchant ship to be ordered from the yard of Alexander Stephen and Sons at Linthouse in Glasgow. She was completed in October 1968 by which time the yard was part of Upper Clyde Shipbuilders. She was delivered to Port Line Ltd and followed her sister **Port Chalmers** into service, being the largest vessels of their type in the world at this time. These were twin-screw shipls with a service speed of 21.5 knots and could accommodate twelve passengers. At 612 feet in length the **Port Caroline** was powered by a pair of 6-cylinder Sulzer engines totalling 26000bhp. She was designed to carry two tiers of containers on deck and her cargo handling gear consisted of seven derricks and five 5-ton cranes. She is seen arriving at Avonmouth in fine weather on 30 March 1973. By 1978 Port Line had become an integral part of parent company Cunard who themselves had been bought out by Trafalgar House Investments six years earlier. The **Port Caroline** and her sister **Port Chalmers** transferred to Brocklebank Line in 1982, becoming **Matra** and **Manaar** respectively. With this move, the much-loved Port Line fleet finally disappeared. The **Port Caroline** became the **Golden Dolphin** in 1983, and passed to Shanghai breakers by April 1985.

(John Wiltshire)

We start by looking at some examples of traditional cargo liners and also a number of cargo ships which were built to carry some refrigerated goods in addition to general cargo. The Federal Steam Navigation Company was formed in 1895 and was taken over by the New Zealand Shipping Company in 1912. Both passed to P&O Line in 1916 and the main service operated until 1973, was from Australia and New Zealand to UK ports such as London, Cardiff and Avonmouth. From 1919 many voyages would transit the Suez Canal. The *Dorset* was 10108 grt and had the distinction of being the final steam ship to be delivered to either Federal or New

Zealand Shipping Company, motor ships having being introduced as early as 1929. At a cost of £621,000 she was a product of Alexander Stephen and Sons Ltd, Glasgow and was delivered on 26 November 1949. The *Dorset* had five cargo holds which included 402900 cubic feet of refrigerated space. She is seen arriving at Cardiff in this view dating from 29 May 1971. Federal had become part of P&O's General Cargo Division in 1971, and the *Dorset* was to be sold to Eckhardt of Hamburg in 1971 for scrap, and then sold on for eventual breaking up at the Golden Horn near Istanbul in August 1972.

(John Wiltshire)

The **Romanic** started life as Royal Mail Line's *Drina* in 1944, and was one of four similar vessels constructed for this company by Harland and Wolff Ltd at Belfast. The other three ships in this series were the **Deseado** of 1942, the **Darro** of 1943 and the **Durango**, also of 1944. Royal Mail Lines became part of Furness Withy and Co in 1965, whereupon the *Drina* was transferred to Shaw Savill and Albion Co Ltd the same year becoming the **Romanic**. Her sistership **Durango** followed in 1966 to become the **Ruthenic**. Despite their age, these ships had a large refrigerated capacity, making them useful additions to the fleet. The **Romanic** was a twin-screw motor ship with an overall length 469 feet, and with five holds served by a mixture of 5 and 10-ton derricks. A notable feature was the prominent goalpost mast forward. Her main power plant consisted of two 6-cylinder 2-stroke Harland & Wolff diesels giving her a speed of 15 knots. She was of closed shelterdeck construction with a gross tonnage of 9785. As the *Drina* she had accommodation for twelve passengers. She is seen at Cardiff on 7 August 1966 berthed in the Roath Dock. Her stay with Shaw Savill was to be brief, as in July 1968 she arrived at Kaohsiung for scrapping.

(John Wiltshire)

Ordered for the Australia services, the **Laurentic** and her sister the **Zealandic** were delivered in 1965 to Shaw Savill and Albion Co Ltd, London. The **Laurentic** was built by Vickers Ltd at Newcastle-upon-Tyne and her maiden voyage took her from London to Fiji and New Zealand via the Panama Canal. At 7964 grt she was 481 feet in length with an overall beam of 66 feet. She had four refrigerated holds with some general cargo space, and two deep tanks suitable for vegetable oils. Cargo handling gear consisted of a pair of 3-ton Clark-Chapman electric cranes, ten conventional derricks and an impressive 30-ton Stülcken derrick. Her main engine was an 8-cylinder Clark & NEM-built Sulzer of 13100bhp, installed in a very modern and highly automated engine room. The **Laurentic** is seen on the Britannia repair quay in Cardiff's Roath Basin on 1 October 1973. She was sold for further trading to Greek owners in 1980 as the **Spartan Reefer**, and on to Pakistani breakers at Gadani Beach in early 1984.

(John Wiltshire)

The Port Line can be traced back as far as 1914 when the Commonwealth and Dominion Line was formed. Cunard took over this company two years later, and the vessels eventually gained their new owner's funnel markings, the Port Line title first appearing in 1937. Port Line operated some very fine-looking refrigerated cargo liners, all of which were motor vessels in the post-war years. Many of these were built by Harland & Wolff Ltd, usually at Belfast, and the larger ships tended to be of twin-screw arrangement. The **Port Launceston** was a splendid single-screw example, completed in November 1957 at the Belfast yard of Harland & Wolff. She was 10225 grt and of closed shelterdeck design. The **Port Launceston** had five cargo holds and had passenger accommodation for ten. A similar ship, the **Port Invercargill** was delivered the following year and would only see nine years service. She was less fortunate being one of the ships stranded in the Bitter Lakes along the Suez Canal, from 1967 until 1975, whereupon she was sold. The **Port Launceston** is seen at Cardiff on 7 April 1977, and later that year became the **United Vantage** under the Singapore flag. Like so many fine ships, she passed to Taiwanese breakers at Kaohsiung, in this case in early 1980.

(John Wiltshire)

The **Tasmania Star** was a refrigerated cargo liner completed in 1950 for Blue Star Line Ltd, by Cammell Laird & Co Ltd of Birkenhead. She was of open shelterdeck design with seven holds (five refrigerated), and a gross tonnage of 12065. Blue Star Line commissioned four similar "Dominion boats" in the 1950s. The **Tasmania Star** and near sistership **Auckland Star** of 1958, were single-screw steam ships. The other pair, the **Adelaide Star** and **Wellington Star** of 1950 and 1952 respectively, built by John Brown on the Clyde, were twin-screw motor vessels. The **Tasmania** **Star** could accommodate up to twelve passengers, and would have been visiting Cardiff with a cargo of dairy produce and meat from New Zealand and possibly Australia. She is seen on 24 July 1972. Her main machinery consisted of three turbines assembled by Cammell Laird with double-reduction gearing and an output of 16000shp. She was sold in late 1975 to Gi Yuen Steel Enterprise Co of Kaohsiung and broken up.

(John Wiltshire)

The **Cap San Diego** was the last vessel in a series of six slightly more unorthodox looking cargo ships built in 1961/2 for West German owner Hamburg-Sudamerikanische of Hamburg. She came from the yard of Deutsche Werft AG, Hamburg in March 1962, and was a partially-refrigerated vessel with accommodation for twelve passengers. She was built for the South American trade, and was to become known as one of the "White Swans of the South Atlantic". The **Cap San Diego** was 9998 grt and her hull was strengthened for operation in ice. Her main engine was a 9-cylinder MAN of 11600bhp and a speed of 19 knots was achievable. She is seen on the New Waterway on 21 June 1980. Having been superseded by container ships, these attractive ships were sold off, and in 1982 the **Cap San Diego** became the **San Diego** for Hansamerica SA (Ybarra Line) under the Panamanian flag. Briefly, in 1986, she became the **Sangria** for Hong Kong owners, before returning to her home port of Hamburg later the same year. She reverted to her original name, having been saved from the breakers by the City of Hamburg who had purchased her as a museum ship. In 2011 she is still preserved at her berth in the German city, and has put to sea on a number of occasions.

(The late Les Ring)

The Gothenburg yard of Eriksbergs Mekaniska Verkstad, built twelve similar partially-refrigerated cargo ships in 1966/67 for both Swedish and Norwegian fleets. The **Hondo** was the first of these distinctive looking ships with their machinery and accommodation located aft. She was launched on 20 January 1966 and completed in the following May for the Swedish East Asiatic Co, who then went on to take the **Hokkaido** followed by the **Hirado** and **Hakone** in 1967. The **Hondo** had a gross tonnage of 10889 and had five main cargo holds as well as cargo-oil tanks. Cargo handling gear included seven electric ASEA cranes and a 60-ton derrick. Her main engine was a B&W assembled by the shipyard with an output of 18000bhp giving the **Hondo** a speed of 18 knots. Her most distinctive feature was her twin exhaust uptakes. In 1978 she was transferred to Broströms Rederi AB, and this is how we see her on 16 April 1979 on the New Waterway. In 1980 she was sold to Afromar Inc of Greece and renamed **Sifnos**. She was despatched for scrapping at Alang during 1994.

(C C Beazley)

Ellerman Line's first motor ship with the machinery situated three-quarters aft was the *City of Melbourne* of 1959. This design was refined several times and as a result the *City of Canberra* of 1961 and 10543 grt, was a much neater looking vessel. She was designed for her owner's trans-Pacific service between America and Australia and was partially-refrigerated. She had five holds, all with upper and lower tween decks and also deep tanks suitable for the carriage of vegetable oil or latex. Her builder Barclay, Curle & Co Ltd of Glasgow installed a 9-cylinder Sulzer type engine of 11700bhp giving her a speed of about 18 knots. At fourteen years of age the *City of Canberra* still makes a fine sight in the New Waterway on 11 July 1975. Ellerman Lines sold her for further trading in 1977, whereupon she became the *Tasgold* of Tasman Gold Shipping Pte Ltd, Singapore and managed by Reefer Lines Pte Ltd, also of Singapore. Two years later she met her end, being broken up on the beaches at Kaohsiung, having been run ashore on 10 November 1979.

(C C Beazley)

Houlder Bros had been trading from the UK to the River Plate region of South America since 1881, and many of the vessels used carried a small number of passengers. The *Royston Grange* was completed for Houlder Line Ltd (Houlder Bros & Co Ltd), London in December 1959 by Hawthorn, Leslie (SB) Ltd at Hebburn, and had a grt of 10262. Her main machinery consisted of two double-reduction geared steam turbines assembled by her builder, which gave her a speed of 16 knots. Steam for the turbines was supplied by two Foster Wheeler water-tube boilers. She had six holds and her chilled cargo capacity was 439,000 cubic feet. Accommodation for twelve first-class passengers was situated at boat deck level, and a swimming pool was also provided. A sistership, **Hardwicke Grange**, was completed in March 1961 by the same yard. On 11 May 1972 and in thick fog, the **Royston Grange** collided with the Liberian flag tanker **Tien Chee** (12500grt/55) 35 miles south west of Montevideo, Uruguay. She was en route to the UK laden with a cargo of frozen beef and butter. A fierce fire engulfed both vessels and all on board the **Royston Grange** were lost. Her hulk was later towed to Spain to be broken up, and arrived at Barcelona on 20 May 1974. In happier days we see her on the Thames in August 1969.

(C C Beazley)

In this view we see the **Brasilia Star** underway on the New Waterway on a fine 1 November 1979, her trading days nearly over. Her large funnel with the unmistakable Blue Star markings seems to dominate this image. She was built for Blue Star Line Ltd in 1957 as the **Queensland Star** by Fairfield SB & Eng Co Ltd of Govan, and had a pair of 5-cylinder Doxford engines driving twin screws. With a gross tonnage of 9911 and an overall length of 511 feet, she had 584,692 cubic feet of insulated cargo space. Like her near sistership **Rockhampton Star**, she was built for the Australia and New Zealand trade, and she could take up to six passengers in en-suite cabins. She became the **Brasilia Star** in 1972 when she was transferred to the South American run. This change took place at Cardiff, and as the **Brasilia Star** she set sail for Buenos Aires on 14 June that year. She later reverted to **Queensland Star** once again in 1977, and her final guise with Blue Star was from 1978 until the end of 1979, as the **Brasilia Star** yet again. She was sold to Taiwanese breakers in December 1979 for scrap, and arrived at Kaohsiung in January 1980.

(John Wiltshire collection)

The origins of the Lamport and Holt Line can be traced back as far as 1845, with steamships sailing from the UK to Brazil, Uruguay and Argentina by 1866. In 1944 Lamport and Holt was purchased by the Vestey Group who owned Blue Star Line. Thereafter it was not unusual for ships to be transferred between fleets. The **Roland** was purchased from Blue Star Line in 1968. She had been launched as **Bolton Castle** by Alexander Stephen & Sons Ltd of Glasgow and completed for Blue Star as the **Dunedin Star** in September 1950. Her gross tonnage was 7322 and she was a partially-refrigerated steam ship with three double-reduction steam turbines of 8800shp. In 1956, her No 2 and 3 lower holds were converted to carry refrigerated goods. As the **Roland** she was employed virtually exclusively on the UK to River Plate and Brazil service from 1968 to 1975. She was a regular visitor to South Wales, and we see her here arriving at Barry in tranquil seas on 31 December 1972. It is thought she had been diverted from the Mersey. Without doubt her most distinguishing feature is her funnel which stands at 46 feet. Despite her age, she was sold in 1975 to Cypriot owners and became the **Jessica**. She made her way to Gadani Beach for breaking up in June 1978.

(Nigel Jones)

New Zealand Shipping's **Turakina** is seen underway in Otago Harbour inward bound to Dunedin on 25 December 1970. She is wearing the funnel colours of Crusader Shipping. This was a joint venture between Shaw Savill, Blue Star, New Zealand Shipping and Port Line established in 1957 to run a refrigerated service between New Zealand and Japan. The **Turakina** was a "one off" vessel for her owner, having only four hatches, and was New Zealand Shipping Co's contribution to the Crusader Shipping venture. She was launched on 26 February 1960 from the South Dock yard of Bartram & Sons Ltd at Sunderland and completed in the following September. The **Turakina** was a 17-knot ship powered by an 8-cylinder Sulzer diesel of 10400bhp and had an overall length of 455 feet. Her name is taken from that of a small Maori village on the Turakina River to the south of Whanganui city on New Zealand's North Island. Crusader Shipping was a loss making venture, from its formation until it was wound up in 1972. The **Turakina** eventually passed to P&O's General Cargo Division in 1973, and was sold in 1978. Initially she became the **Patricia U** of Uiterwyk Line, Monrovia, and later the **Gulf Reefer** under the Greek flag from 1982. Her final years were as the Maltese flag **Sines** from 1985 until she was broken up at Huangpu in China during early 1986.

(The late Alwyn Macmillan - Chris Howell collection)

The refrigerated cargo liner **Port New Plymouth** was another twin-screw motor ship for Port Line Ltd of London, and the final example to be constructed for them by Swan, Hunter & Wigham Richardson, in this case at their Wallsend shipyard. She was completed in October 1960 with a gross tonnage of 13085, and had accommodation for twelve passengers. Of six-hold layout, her cargo handling gear included a 75-ton derrick. Main engines consisted of a pair of 6-cylinder Sulzer diesels assembled by the Wallsend Slipway, which gave her a speed of 18 knots. When delivered she was considered to be the fifth largest refrigerated ship in the world. In 1971 she undertook the final sailing from Auckland in New Zealand on the Montreal, Australia and New Zealand Line run, to the east coast of the USA. In 1979 management of the **Port New Plymouth** passed to Cunard Shipping Services, and later that year she was sold to Panamanian flag interests as the **Plymouth**. However, after just one voyage, she was sold for breaking up at Kaohsiung in Taiwan, arriving there on 3 October 1979. Here we see her in Otago Harbour, New Zealand, outward bound from Dunedin on 2 April 1977.

(The late Alwyn Macmillan - Chris Howell collection)

The **Southampton Castle** was the first of a pair of very distinctive fast refrigerated cargo and mail ships for Union Castle Mail SS Co Ltd, London. Having been launched on 20 October 1964 by HRH Princess Alexandra, she was completed in the following May. Her builders Swan, Hunter and Wigham Richardson of Wallsend then went on to complete the **Good Hope Castle** by the end of 1965. These twin-screw ships of 10538 grt were powered by a pair of 8-cylinder Sulzer engines of 34720bhp which would enable them to reach up to 25 knots, and in 1965 they were claimed to be the fastest diesel-powered cargo ships afloat. They had seven holds nearly two-thirds of which was refrigerated, and could carry a mixture of fruit and chilled or frozen meat, as well as 60,000 gallons of wine in special tanks. In 1967 accommodation for twelve passengers was added by Cammell Laird at Birkenhead. The **Southampton Castle** was photographed on a sunny day in October 1972 at Southampton, her huge funnel being a most remarkable feature of this motor vessel. She continued to trade for Union Castle until October 1977 and in February 1978 was sold to Costa Armatori SpA of Italy, and renamed **Franca C**. Upon sale in 1983 to Court Shipping Co Ltd of Malta she became simply **Franca**, and was initially destined for breakers at Alang by the end of that year. However, on 19 January 1984, the former **Southampton Castle** arrived at Dalian in north-east China, for breaking up.

(Derek Chaplin)

Probably the most common type of cargo for the pure reefer was and still is bananas. This perishable fruit which we take for granted, has to be transported at a constant temperature to ensure it is in peak condition when it reaches the market place. Here follows a selection of vessels employed in the banana trade. W Bruns and Co of Hamburg regularly chartered vessels to Geest Industries Ltd in the 1960s and the *Brunstal* of 1959 is seen at Barry on 5 August 1969. She was one of a pair of refrigerated ships acquired by W Bruns in 1966 from I/S Freezer of Oslo, part of the Torvald Klaveness group, and had previously sailed as the *Baleares*. She was built by Verschure & Co's Schps, Amsterdam, and had a gross tonnage of 2825. Her main engine was an 8-cylinder MAN of 5200bhp and she was 377 feet in length. The *Brunstal* had three cargo holds with four hatches served by eight derricks. She became the *Salta* in 1970 under the Norwegian flag and later the *Gema* in 1977 for Panamanian flag owners. Reverting to the name *Salta* in 1985, she was broken up at Porto Alegre in 1986. Of note on the quayside are the railway banana vans, still used at this time to transport the fruit away from the port.

(John Wiltshiire)

Between 1964 and 1966 Geest Industries took delivery of four modern ships for the UK to Caribbean and Windward Islands trade. A second quartet gradually replaced the initial four from 1972, the third in this new series being the **Geestland** of 1972. All four were constructed by Scotts SB Co (1969) Ltd of Greenock on the Clyde and were capable of 21 knots. The **Geestland** was launched on 21 February 1972 and would eventually be followed into service by the **Geeststar**. She was 5871 grt with an insulated cargo capacity of 9718 cubic metres. Her cargo gear consisted of three electric cranes and six derricks, whilst her main engine was a 6-cylinder Sulzer of 12000bhp. As with the earlier four vessels, there would be accommodation for twelve passengers. On the afternoon tide of 1 July 1973, the **Geestland** is making her way into Barry in very pleasant weather conditions. She gave her owner fourteen years service, after which she became the **Starland** in 1986 under the Cypriot flag and finally **Valparaiso Reefer** in 1990. She arrived at Bhatiary in Bangladesh on 10 July 1994 for breaking up.

(Nigel Jones)

Geest Industries operated out of Barry from the 1960s until 1982, when the promise of improved facilities led to a move across the Bristol Channel to Avonmouth. Following labour problems at the latter port, Geest returned to Barry in 1984, but the delivery of a pair of larger vessels in 1993 meant that a move to Southampton was inevitable. These two new 20-knot vessels were the **Geest St. Lucia** and **Geest Dominica**, products of Danyard A/S, Frederikshavn and registered in the Bahamas. They were modern ships and quite different from the previous Geest vessels. At 13077 grt and 519 feet in length, the **Geest St. Lucia** was designed for palletised cargoes and had 16990 cubic metres of insulated cargo space. She could also carry up to 439 twenty foot containers of which 170 could be refrigerated. The **Geest St. Lucia** is seen here at Southampton on 5 May 1993 when new, berthed at the Windward Terminal. In 1997 Geest sold their interests in the banana trade to a consortium including Fyffes, and the two 1993-built ships became the **St. Lucia** and **Dominica** respectively and initially gained Fyffes colours. As the **St. Lucia** she went on to work in the Lauritzen Cool pool, and from 2007 became part of the NYKCool AB pool. She took the name **Autumn Wind** in 2008, still under the Bahamas flag.

(John Wiltshire)

The **Jamaica Planter** was launched on 10 August 1959 for the Jamaica Banana Producers Steamship Co Ltd, London by Lithgows Ltd of Port Glasgow. Her owners can be traced back to 1929 with the formation of the Jamaica Direct Fruit Line who began operating four vessels dating from 1910/11. The **Jamaica Planter** was a steam powered vessel built for the West Indies to UK service. She was a fine-looking ship of 6159grt and 445 feet overall length, and had passenger accommodation for twelve. She could carry approximately 1900 tons of bananas in her holds and tween decks, but was also suitable for the shipment of exotic fruits such as mango and paw paw. Her Pametrada-type geared turbines built by D Rowan & Co Ltd had an output of 7000shp, and gave her a service speed of 17 knots. She is seen here well away from her normal haunts, berthed in the Roath Basin at Cardiff on 18 February 1973. Her visit to South Wales was for drydocking. The **Jamaica Planter** was sold the following year to Singapore owners and renamed **Vine Fruit**. She was broken up by Lien Hong Iron and Steel Works of Kaohsiung, Taiwan, arriving there on 19 August 1976.

(John Wiltshire)

Elders and Fyffes was formed in 1902, and by 1910 was under the control of the United Fruit Company of the United States. Services from the UK were operated to Central America and the Caribbean, and in particular Jamaica. The *Camito* was a 1956-built passenger cargo ship of 8687 grt from the yard of Alexander Stephen & Sons Ltd of Linthouse on the Clyde. She was lauched for Elders and Fyffes on 27 March 1956 and completed by November 1956. She was similar in most respects to the earlier *Golfito* of 1949, and had a length of 447 feet. Both ships were employed on the service to Jamaica, Barbados and Trinidad and would carry a variety of general cargo on the outward run. The *Camito* could accommodate an impressive 96 first class passengers on three decks. Facilities included a cinema and a swimming pool. Her banana payload was quoted as being approximately 140,000 stems in four refrigerated holds. She was twin-screw with a speed of 17.5 knots, and like many of Elders and Fyffes' ships, her machinery was steam turbine. We see the *Camito* laid up at No101 berth Southampton on 11 August 1972, her trading days being just about over. She was eventually to depart for breakers in Taiwan, reaching Kaohsiung on 3 April 1973.

(John Wiltshire)

A series of five small motor ships was constructed for United Fruit's Honduran subsidiary, Empresa Hondurena de Vapores SA by Bremer Vulkan of Vegesack. The first of these was the **Leon** which was completed in September 1952. She was followed by the **Lempa**, **Almirante**, **Aragon** and finally the **Atenas** in 1955. The **Leon** was a closed shelterdeck ship of 2816 grt, her hull being 340 feet in length with three holds served by seven derricks. She was twin-screw being powered by two 5-cylinder Bremer Vulkan-built MAN diesels situated aft. In 1959 the **Leon** and the **Lempa** were transferred within the United Fruit group to Surrey Shipping Company of Hamilton for use on the Southampton to Caribbean service, and were renamed **Box Hill** and **Leith Hill** respectively. In 1964 both vessels were lengthened by 29 feet and this gave the **Leon** a new grt of 3245. In 1966 both ships returned to the Honduras fleet and took up their original names once again. As such, we see the **Leon** visiting Cardiff for drydocking on 21 November 1977. She would be sold to Asalvamentos Y Desguaces on 13 September 1980, for breaking up at San Juan de Nieva in Spain.

(John Wiltshire)

The final steam-powered ships built for the United Fruit group of companies were half a dozen elegant single-screw cargo ships from the Bremer Vulkan yard. All were destined for the Surrey Shipping Co Ltd and registered in London, and would trade worldwide for Elders and Fyffes. The first of these vessels which became known as the "T class", was the **Tenadores**, delivered in February 1960. The **Tucurinca**, delivered in 1962, was the last of the six to arrive. She is seen here on the New Waterway on 10 July 1976, her side doors clearly visible. The 6738 grt **Tucurinca** could take five passengers, and was powered by two double-reduction steam turbines of 8500shp by AB De Lavals and could maintain 18 knots. She was designed to carry 60,000 stems of bananas and could also accommodate boxed fruit, chilled meat and general cargo in her four holds. Commencing in 1965, all of these ships eventually moved over to the Honduran flag, operating for Empresa Hondurena de Vapores SA, with the **Tucurinca** doing so in 1978. All six "T class" vessels were to have relatively short careers being steam turbine, and therefore very uneconomical to operate. They were all sold for scrap to Taiwanese breakers between December 1979 and February 1980, with the **Tucurinca** arriving at Kaohsiung on 31 January 1980.

(C C Beazley)

Newport had first received imports of bananas before World War 2 and this recommenced for a while in 1946. With the arrival of Jamaica Producers in 1980, many different refrigerated ships would start to arrive at the port. Typical of many Japanese-built reefers completed in the 1980s and 1990s was the **Lilyeverett** of 1993. She was completed in July of that year for Everett-Orient Line by Kitanihon Zosen KK of Hachinohe and had a grt of 7800. She was typically, of all-aft layout, and had four cargo holds of total refrigerated capacity 13303 cubic feet, and served by eight derricks. The **Lilyeverett** was an 18-knot ship powered by a 6-cylinder Mitsubishi engine of 8640bhp, built by Akasaka Diesels Ltd. She is seen at Newport on 25 August 1996, and a large number of containers are visible on deck. In 1997 she became the **Logan** for Kaon Ltd and sailing under the Liberian flag. She is believed to be still in service in 2011 under the name **Hai Feng 618** and managed by China National Fisheries Corp, which seems to imply that she may now be operating as a fish carrier.

(Nigel Jones)

What was formerly an iron ore berth at Newport docks was rebuilt in 1980 into the new terminal for the import of Jamaican bananas. A new generation of ships would start to arrive at the port and included vessels like the Japanese flag **Caribbean Maru**. She had been launched on 10 October 1978 by the Kurushima Dock Co Ltd of Onishi in Japan for owners Toko Kaiun KK of Kobe. She was very typical of reefers built in Japan in the late 1970s and 1980s, and had a grt of 10504. She entered service in 1979 as a pure reefer with an insulated cargo capacity of 12743 cubic metres, spread across four holds. She was a 19.5 knot ship with a 17100bhp, 9-cylinder main engine built by Kawasaki Heavy Industries under licence from MAN. This view of the **Caribbean Maru** at the Jamaica Producers terminal was taken in wintery sun on 3 January 1987. She became the **Swan Bay** in 1989 for Santiago Shipping Inc of Norway, and continued to visit Newport in this guise. Her final name change was to **Pietari Frost** in 2004 under the St Vincent and Grenadines flag, and sailing for Clearwater Marine. She was scrapped at Chittagong in 2008.

(John Wiltshire)

We now look at some elderly and somewhat smaller refrigerated ships in their twilight years. Making a fine sight as she proceeds along the New Waterway on 27 June 1977 is the Greek flag *Evelpis* of 1952. She is trading for Artemision Shipping Co SA of Piraeus. This fascinating ship was built as the *Kadoura* for French owner Cie Maritime des Chargeurs Réunis by J Samuel White & Co Ltd at Cowes on the Isle of Wight. She was a twin-screw banana carrier and intended for the West Africa and Canaries trade. At 3210 grt and 359 feet in length, she had accommodation for twelve first-class passengers and a speed of 16 knots. The *Kadoura* had five holds and four deep tanks and was powered by a pair of 8-cylinder Burmeister and Wain diesels with a combined output of 6500bhp at 165rpm. In 1968 she became the *Asterix* for Gold Star Cia Mar SA under Greek registry and in 1970 gained the name *Evelpis* which she carries in this photograph. The end came in March 1980 with her arrival in Pakistan for breaking up at Gadani Beach.

(The late Les Ring)

Making her final approach to the lock at Cardiff is another refrigerated ship, with a cargo of oranges from Israel. The date is 25 April 1970, and at this time imports of citrus fruit to Cardiff were a regular occurrence. Most, however, arrived in modern ships, usually fully refrigerated "pure reefers". The Norwegian flag **Borealis** was a pleasant exception to the rule, and appears to be in rather good condition for her age. She dates from 1948 and was not a large vessel by any means with a gross tonnage of just 2919. She was launched on 14 October 1947 by Smith's Dock Co Ltd, South Bank near Middlesbrough for Den Norske Middelhavslinje A/S of Olso, with Fred Olsen & Co and Ole R Thoressen as managers. The **Borealis** had an overall length of 364 feet and was powered by a 4-cylinder NE Marine Eng Co diesel giving her a speed of 14 knots. In 1972 she became the **Vikhav** for Sigurd Haavik A/S of Norway, and was broken up at Hong Kong in 1973.

(Nigel Jones)

Seeing out her final years trading in Far Eastern waters, was this German-built vessel, the **Pacific Mulia**. Now flying the Malaysian flag she was operating for Pacific Mulia Senderian Berhad, of Labuan. She had started out being completed in May 1955 by Kieler Howaldtswerke AG of Kiel as the **Ravnefjell** for Norwegian owner A/S Dovrefjell of Oslo. In 1959 she was lengthened from 259 feet to 297 feet, and therefore her gross tonnage increased from 1661 to 1937. She was an open shelterdeck motor vessel with accommodation for four passengers. In 1967 she became the **Arta** under the Greek flag and finally the **Pacific Mulia** in 1980. She is seen at anchor and working a bagged cargo in Singapore Roads on 20 June 1980, and it is quite likely that by this time her days carrying refrigerated goods were over. The later addition of a new section of hull, forward of her accommodation is fairly easy to see. As **Pacific Mulia**, she was broken up at Kaohsiung in 1985.

(Nigel Jones)

The New Waterway never seemed to disappoint the observer and photographer alike, and just when shipping activity seemed to be fairly quiet, something interesting would come along. On 21 June 1976 the Tunisian-owned **Monastir** was no exception, an unusual vessel in many respects. Her profile was quite unlike a conventional refrigerated ship. She was owned by Cie Tunisienne de Navigation of Tunis, and had been built in the United States in 1947 as the **Saint Pierre** by Tampa SB Co of Tampa, Florida. She became the **Monastir** in 1962, and was officially classed as a part bulk wine carrier of 2934 grt. She was a twin-screw vessel capable of 16.5 knots. Her bridge and main accommodation were situated amidships, while her machinery was placed aft. Her demise was intended to be at the breakers yard, but this was not to happen. During October 1979, while being towed from Piraeus to breakers at Castellon in Spain, the **Monastir** broke loose and was wrecked.

(The late Les Ring)

Citrus fruit such as oranges and grapefruit was imported to Cardiff on a seasonal basis from Israel in late winter and spring and South Africa during our early summer. Maritime Fruit Carriers of Haifa, Israel operated a fleet of modern reefers from the mid-1960s. The first class of vessel were the "Cores", built in three different Norwegian yards between 1964 and 1971. An initial group of four ships included the **Lemoncore** of 1964 followed by the **Mangocore**, **Avocadocore** and **Bananacore** in 1965. All four were sailing under the Israeli flag, and, being partly financed by the government of that country, had limited military features. The

Lemoncore is seen discharging at Cardiff on 16 March 1975, her goalpost masts forward of her accommodation being a distinguishing feature of this class. She was 8139 grt and built by A/S Bergens M/V of Bergen. She had four fully refrigerated holds served by twelve derricks. A further twelve similar "Core" reefers were built for Maritime Fruit Carriers between 1968 and 1971 (see also page 47). The **Lemoncore** was sold to the United Fruit Co in 1976 upon the collapse of Maritime Fruit Carriers, and became the **Omoa** under the Honduras flag. She was eventually broken up at Shanghai in 1985.

(John Wiltshire)

The South African Marine Corporation came into being in 1947 when it began trading with a trio of Victory-type ships. In the early 1960s they ordered four refrigerated ships to cater for the expanding fruit exporting trade in South Africa. Delivery of these ships began with the *Langkloof* in 1963 followed by the *Letaba*, *Drakenstein* and finally the *Tzaneen* in August 1964. All were named after fruit-producing areas in South Africa. The *Langkloof* was built in the Netherlands by the Verolme shipyard, while the other three were completed on the Clyde by Greenock Dockyard Co Ltd. All gained the "S. A." prefix to their names in 1966, and the *S. A. Tzaneen* was by now officially recorded as being owned by Huntley Cook, South Africa (Pty) Ltd, Cape Town. She was an open shelterdeck vessel of 17 knots and gross tonnage of 6837. The *S. A. Tzaneen* was designed to carry packed citrus fruit, apples and pears, deciduous fruit (such as mangos, grapes and peaches) in her six holds, and in addition her number 6 hold could be used for frozen meat. The photographer has captured her in dramatic lighting conditions off Penarth Head after sailing from Cardiff on 4 July 1974. In 1977 she reverted to the name *Tzaneen* and changed on two subsequent occasions, before becoming the *Papagayo Universal* in 1979. This change involved a re-flagging of the ship to avoid trade restrictions imposed on South African vessels at this time. In 1982 she took her final name, *Asia Freezer* under the Panamanian flag, and was broken up at Chittagong in 1985.

(Nigel Jones)

The United Fruit Co ordered eighteen steam turbine vessels to replace war losses, and nine of these would be twin-screw vessels of the "Fra Berlenga" class. One of these ships was the **Limon** of 7074 gross tons, which was completed in May 1945 for United Mail SS Co of New York, a United Fruit Co subsidiary. Her builder was the Gulf SB Corp of Chickasaw, Alabama, and she was 433 feet in length and 61 feet in the beam, with accommodation for twelve passengers. The **Limon** had four steam turbines with double-reduction gearing manufactured by the DeLaval Steam Turbine Co. In 1970 along with three similar ships, she was transferred to the associated Dutch fleet, NV Caraibische Scheepvaart Mij of Rotterdam as the **Talamanca** by which time her grt was recorded as 6729. On 1 May 1977 she is seen off Penarth Head and making some fine smoke, having sailed from Cardiff after discharging a cargo of citrus fruit. She was now embarking upon her final voyage to the breakers yard. The **Talamanca** would sail to the Far East via the Panama Canal, arriving at Kaohsiung on 7 July 1977.

(Andrew Wiltshire)

We shall now look at some reefers sailing for Swedish operator Sven Salén who entered the shipping business in 1915 and bought his first refrigerated ship in 1941. Over the years Salén Rederierna also chartered a large number of vessels, and so it was not unusual to see a reefer anywhere in the world wearing Salén's funnel markings of dark blue with a white S motif. The **Australic** was completed in March 1965 for Per Carlsson of Gothenburg and was 8253 grt. Her builder was Eriksbergs M/V A/B also of Gothenburg and she was designed with very graceful lines, for the shipment of perishables including bananas, fruit and meat. Her four holds were insulated with fibre-glass and were served by four electric cranes which spoilt her otherwise attractive profile. Her main engine was an Uddevallavarvet-built B&W diesel of 10000bhp, giving her a speed of 19 knots. The **Australic** went on to become the **Ionian Reefer** in 1978 for Progress Compania Naviera SA flying the Greek flag and then the **Reefer Tiger** in 1985 under the Panamanian flag. Her final years in service were as the **Reefer Turbo** from 1986 until she was broken up at Bombay in late 1993. We see her on the New Waterway on 4 September 1978.

(The late Les Ring)

Salén went on to become the largest operator of reefers in the world and introduced a number of groups of new ships into its own fleet. The **San Bruno** of 1967 was a classic pure reefer, one of four similar ships built by Eriksbergs M/V A/B of Gothenburg. Two others were the **San Blas** of 1967 and **San Benito** of 1968, which were also completed for Salénrederierna A/B fleet under the Swedish flag. By 1979 the **San Bruno** was recorded as being owned by Trans-Swedish Shipping Inc of Manila, and flying the Philippine flag. She had more modern lines than the **Australic** on page 26, and features a bulbous bow, a transom stern as well as a flume stabilisation system. She was 8223 tons gross and had four holds, which in this case can be cooled down to -22°C. The main engine was a 7-cylinder B&W built under licence by the shipyard. A controllable-pitch propeller was fitted and a speed of 20.5 knots was attainable. Once again the New Waterway provides the setting for this view taken on 14 July 1983. That same year the **San Bruno** was to be renamed **Malayan Venture** for the same owners, and would sail for a further two years until broken up in China in 1985.

(John Wiltshire collection)

Probably the best known Salén reefers were the eight strong "Snow" class from the French shipyard Chantiers Nav de La Ciotat and delivered in the early 1970s. These were modern and attractive ships with a speed of nearly 23 knots and overall length of 568 feet. The first to be completed was the **Snow Flower** in February 1972 and all eight were active with the delivery in April 1974 of the **Snow Hill**. Here we see the **Snow Ball** of 1973 and 10409 grt on the New Waterway on 6 July 1975. She has five holds of 17319 cubic metres capacity, served by eight 5-ton cranes, and can also accommodate a number of vehicles below deck, and 16 containers on deck. Her 8-cylinder Sulzer engine of 23200bhp drives a controllable-pitch propeller. By 1981 all eight of the "Snow" ships were flying the Red Ensign and were operating for Salen UK Ship Management. The **Snow Ball** was sold in 1981 taking three names until becoming the **Savona Star** in 1985 for Miralta Corp under the Panamanian flag, and with Wallem Ship Management Ltd as managers. In 1988 she passed to Ginetta Shpg SA, Nassau as the **Santiago Star** and then **Snow Cape** in 1996. Reverting to **Santiago Star** in 2000, she continued to sail for Ginetta Shipping until sold for breaking up at Chittagong, arriving there in August 2006.

(C C Beazley)

A further class of advanced pure reefers for Salén comprised the six "Winter" ships. These functional-looking vessels lacked the style and character of the "Snow" class, but were in many ways a development of them. They were almost as large but only had four holds and were designed to accommodate multi-pallet loading and had a 240 TEU container capacity, an important advance over the "Snow" class. They were all built in Sweden this time at two associated yards. This photograph depicts the **Winter Moon** sailing from Newport on 9 May 1982, having arrived with a cargo of bananas. She was launched on 9 October 1978 by Götaverken Arendal AB at Gothenburg for owners Salénrederierna A/B, Stockholm. Completed in 1979, she was 11690grt and had a length of 552 feet and a refrigerated capacity of 17143 cubic metres. A 6-cylinder B&W diesel coupled to a controllable-pitch propeller gave her a service speed of 22 knots. Another feature was the installation of a bow-thruster unit. All six "Winter" ships were owned by Zenit Reefer AB (Nordia Shipping) of Gothenburg by 1985 and had gained the "Zenit" prefix to their name in place of "Winter". The **Zenit Moon** reverted to her former name **Winter Moon** later that year. She was sold in 1999 to Alcazar Shipping Corp, Nassau, as **Alcazar Carrier** and flying the Bahamas flag. The first Winter ships to head for the breakers did not do so until 2009. The **Winter Star** was the first followed by the **Winter Sea**. The **Winter Moon** was to end up on breaking beaches at Alang in September 2009. The **Winter Sun** followed in June 2011.

(Danny Lynch)

The Lauritzen family from Esbjerg in Denmark entered the shipping industry in 1888, and upon the outbreak of war in 1914, Ditlev Lauritzen moved back to Copenhagen. A holding company J Lauritzen was created, and in 1932 they purchased their first refrigerated ship. The **Roman Reefer** was the fourth ship in the "Italian Reefer" class, which ran to six vessels commencing with the **Italian Reefer** in 1968. This class of reefer introduced the painting of the vessels' name in large letters on the hull. All of these 23-knot ships were built by Aalborg Værft A/S, a company which Lauritzen had taken over in 1937. The **Roman Reefer** was completed in November 1970 for J Lauritzen A/S of Esbjerg with a gross tonnage of 6009 and an overall length of 477 feet. She had four holds with a number of tween decks, and her cargo-handling gear consisted of four distinctive Velle type derricks of 5-ton capacity. Her main machinery consisted of an 8-cylinder Burmeister and Wain, slow-speed diesel of 15000bhp. She is seen on 7 April 1983 on the New Waterway. The **Roman Reefer** became the **Mango Reefer** trading for Kara Shipping SA under the Bahamas flag in 1992, and was broken up at Alang in 1999.

(John Wiltshire collection)

Lauritzen's vessels could usually be distinguished by their red hulls, and the reefers were good examples of this. The **Argentinean Reefer** was launched in 1940 by Aalborg Værft A/S and completed in January 1941. However, due to the outbreak of war, and the German occupation of Denmark she was laid up at Copenhagen and not commissioned until July 1945. Her maiden voyage was from Aalborg to Le Havre with food supplies for the US Army. At 2826 tons gross, she was a small twin-screw vessel with a turn of speed at just over 15 knots. Twenty years later in 1965, she is seen at Auckland loading meat, and at this time Lauritzen had a service exporting meat and fruit from New Zealand to Japan. She arrived at Copenhagen in June 1967 to lay up for disposal and a year later was sold to the Union SS Co of New Zealand. After an overhaul at Aalborg she was renamed **Taveuni**. In 1972 she became the **Wan Lee** under the Panamanian flag but only undertook one voyage as such, and she was broken up at Kaohsiung, arriving there on 23 January 1973. The first of three new motor reefers for Lauritzen arrived in 1953, in the shape of the **Mexican Reefer**, a 3947grt, twin-screw, 18 knot ship. Four larger vessels were also completed by the Aalborg yard between 1958 and 1962 and included the **Arabian Reefer** and **Chilean Reefer**.

(Mike Cornwall - Chris Howell collection)

A pair of fast reefers was acquired by J Lauritzen in 1981 for use by subsidiary company Frigg Shipping Ltd and under the Bahamas flag. The two vessels, the **Blumenthal** of 1974 and the **Bremerhaven** of 1975 had been trading for West German owner Scipio and Co of Bremen, and were to gain the traditional names **Belgian Reefer** and **Brazilian Reefer** respectively. The **Belgian Reefer** was completed by Howaldtswerke-Deutsche Werft of Hamburg with a gross tonnage of 8729. She had a pair of 18-cylinder medium-speed Blohm and Voss (Pielstick) diesels of 23400bhp driving a single controllable-pitch propeller. She is seen here at Bluff, New Zealand in June 1985, and of note is her white hull, not what you would expect to find on a Lauritzen reefer. They were deemed unsuccessful ships, and the pair were sold on in 1986. The **Belgian Reefer** was to become the Cypriot flag **Frio Scandinavia** for Countach Shipping Co Ltd, and later the **Atlantika** in 1989. As is so often the case with reefers, as they change trades and take up new charters etc, further name changes followed. The ship that had started out as the **Blumenthal** ended her days as the **Windfrost** from 1994 until broken up at Alang in 1997.

(Chris Howell)

The next class of reefers for Lauritzen after the "Italian Reefer" series was the "Asian Reefer" class which ran to a total of four ships. They were larger with a gross tonnage of 8874 and 16600 cubic metres of refrigerated capacity in four cargo holds. The **Asian Reefer** and **Balkan Reefer** of 1978 were built in Japan by Hayashikane SB & Eng Co Ltd of Nagasaki. The final pair, the **Canadian Reefer** and **Ecuadorian Reefer** were then completed in 1979 and 1980 by the Aalborg yard in Denmark. The **Balkan Reefer** was also capable of carrying seventy containers and ten passengers, and had a speed of 21 knots. She is nearly 21 years old in this view taken at Walsoorden on 22 June 1999. A notable feature is the very tall funnel clearly visible in this shot. The **Balkan Reefer** was sold in 2002 and passed to Maltese owners Algae Shipping Co Ltd, of Valletta as the **Baltic Sun**. She is believed to be still sailing in 2011.

(Douglas Cromby)

West German shipyards built a considerable number of refrigerated ships including many pure reefers, and not just for German owners. They included many distinctive designs and often incorporating many innovative and advanced features. The *Cap Frio* was built for West German shipowner Hamburg South America Line (Hamburg-Südamerikanische), a company that had been founded in 1871, and which by 1914 was operating over fifty ships. Her builder Lübecker Flender-Werke AG of Lübeck completed her on 15 March 1955 as an open shelter-deck layout, refrigerated cargo ship with a gross tonnage of 5857. She was one of four similar ships delivered to her owner in 1955, the *Cap Blanco* being a near sister while the *Cap Norte* and *Cap Vilano* were slightly larger at 6602 grt. The *Cap Frio* had provision for twelve passengers and was capable of 17 knots. This view of her in November 1969 at Vancouver shows clearly her traditional German lines and also the Hamburg-Süd funnel colours of white with a red top. She became the Greek-owned *Karpathos* in 1971 for Afromar Inc of Piraeus, and was broken up ten years later at Gadani Beach.

(Bernard McCall collection)

Two high-specification reefers, the **Polarlicht** and **Polarstern**, were delivered to Hamburg-Südamerikanische in 1964 (see also page 54). The second vessel was the **Polarstern**, launched on 10 July 1964 by Deutsche Werft AG at Finkenwerder, Hamburg. She was a 4970 grt vessel of 469 feet overall length with four cargo holds and accommodation for just three passengers. Her engine was a 9-cylinder MAN installed in a highly automated engine room that featured bridge control of engine movements. She is seen here manoeuvring in Kings Dock at Swansea as a storm gathers over the hills behind on 4 December 1973. Her visit to Swansea was for drydocking, most probably for an annual survey. The **Polarstern** was sold to the Fyffes Group Ltd in 1974 and became the **Darien** under the British flag. In 1981 she became the **Chion Carrier** for Ichnusa Shipping Corp under the Greek flag before taking two further names in 1984. Firstly as the **Khumbu** and then **Khumbu I** for her journey to Pakistani breakers in December of that year.

(John Wiltshire)

Hamburg-Sudamerikanische continued to be leaders in reefer design when they introduced a class of six very unusual looking ships in 1967. The first example was the **Polar Ecuador**, and the **Polar Colombia** seen here was the third to be completed in March 1968. They were flush-decked vessels with a pair of tall and distinctive funnels, which acted as a mast for the 5-ton derricks serving No 3 hold. All were initially put out on charter to Salén and were used for the transport of both bananas and meat. All six ships were constructed by Blohm and Voss at Steinwerder near Hamburg, and the **Polar Colombia** was 5623grt and 485 feet in length. She had four holds with No3 being between the main superstructure and engine-room. Two 16-cylinder Ottensener Eisenwerk (Pielstick) diesels were geared to a single propeller, and gave her an impressive speed of 22 knots. All were sold for further service but the **Polar Ecuador** and **Polar Brasil** were to be scrapped by 1986. The **Polar Colombia** took a number of different names from 1984, and was the last example to survive, going to Indian ship-breakers at Alang in 1998 as the Cypriot flagged **Miramar**. Here we see her arriving at Barry on 9 June 1979, and by now flying the Liberian flag. She is on charter to Geest, but wearing the funnel markings of Dole Fresh Fruit.

(Bob Allen)

This neat little ship was built in West Germany in 1953 by H C Stülcken Sohn of Hamburg for Italian interests. She was launched as the 2967 grt **Frachina Fasso** for Villian & Fassio Soc Italiana di Nav Mertantile SpA and sailed for them from 1953 until 1957. Ownership then changed to Villian & Fasso e Cia Internazionale di Genova Soc Riunite de Nav Spa until 1970, and still under the Italian flag. At this point she was sold to French-flag interests, Société Navale Caennaise (Anct G Lamy & Co), and who renamed her **Danae**. As such we see her at Cardiff on 9 April 1972 having arrived to discharge apples. She is in desperate need of some fresh white paint. The **Danae** was a 16-knot ship powered by a 7-cylinder MAN diesel of 4670bhp, and she had five holds that were served by ten derricks. In 1974 she became the **Blue Ocean** for Saudi owners Ahmed Mohamed Baaboud and Ahmed Mohamed Baghlaf of Jeddah. As such she was broken up at Gadani Beach in 1981.

(John Wiltshire)

A very well-kept and attractive reefer, the *Tropical Sun* is seen arriving at Newport on 29 June 1980. She is flying the Liberian flag and is owned by Intercontinental Transportation Services Ltd of Monrovia. She was completed in 1968 as the *Brunshausen* for W Bruns of Hamburg and was one of a series of around fourteen similar ships delivered to this fleet between 1963 and 1968. As the *Brunshausen*, she had a gross tonnage of 4623 and was built by Howaldtswerke Hamburg AG of Hamburg, with an overall length of 428 feet, which took into consideration her bulbous bow. Her cargo space consisted of four holds with an insulated capacity of 8646 cubic metres, with additional access by four side doors to both port and starboard. Her main engine was an 8-cylinder MAN of 10500bhp giving her a speed of 20 knots. Of note was that Intercontinental Transportation Services also owned the similar former W Bruns ships, the *Brunskamp*, *Brunsbüttel* and *Brunsrode*. By 1986 the *Tropical Sun* was owned by Mahele Reefer Ltd still under Liberian flag, and carried on to have a lengthy career under this name. She was eventually sold for breaking up at Alang in April 1998, having last sailed for Dole Fresh Fruit International Ltd of Liberia.

(Bob Allen)

Although the French did not build many reefers, some early examples were very elegant and distinctive looking ships. The **Espadon** was no exception and followed the layout of having her No 3 hold as the smallest of the four, between the main accommodation and the engine room. She was launched on 4 January 1962 at Nantes by Ateliers & Chantiers de Nantes (Bretagne-Loire), for shipowner Société Générale de Transports Maritimes, of Marseilles. She was 4731 grt and 378 feet in length with a beam of 52 feet. The **Espadon** was a single-screw vessel, but with two Pielstick main engines giving her a speed of 17 knots. She was sailing for

Cie Fabre, Soc Générale de Transports Maritimes, from 1964 until 1977 when she became **Lethe** under the Liberian flag, and then **Opaline Bay** in 1979. This dramatic shot of her as the **Victoria Reefer** was taken on the Suez Canal on 23 June 1995. By now she was under the Panamanian flag and sailing for Comercio Internacional de Atun SA (COINASA). As such, she regularly loaded perishable cargoes at the Indian Ocean islands of Madagascar and the Seychelles, destined ultimately for Spanish ports. At the impressive age of 42 years, the **Victoria Reefer** was sold for breaking up at Alang in June 2004.

(Nigel Jones)

Another fine-looking French-built reefer was the **Bambara** of 1958. She was completed by SA des Chantiers Réunis Loire-Normandie of Grand Quévilly for Cie de Navigation Fraissenet & Cyprien Fabre, of Marseilles. She traded for them until 1961, when she passed to Société Ivoirienne de Consignation et Armements flying the flag of the Ivory Coast, previously a French colony. In 1966 the title of this fleet changed to Société Ivoirienne de Transports Maritimes (SITRAM), for whom she was trading in this view at Southampton on 10 April 1971. Her port of registry is Abidjan. The **Bambara** was a motor ship powered by a 7-cylinder Burmeister & Wain engine producing 5750bhp at 150rpm and giving her a speed of 18 knots. Her gross tonnage was 4410 and she had an overall length of 378 feet. The **Bambara** had distinctive bipod masts, and in addition to 5500 cubic metres of refrigerated space, she had special tanks for carriage of wine. Her first change of name came in 1973 when she was sold to Saudi Lines of Jeddah as the **Al Qaseem**. In 1981 she was converted into a livestock carrier which gave her a new gross tonnage of 2575. In 1986 she was renamed **Romeo** for a trip to the breakers at Gadani Beach.

(Nigel Jones)

French shipowner Cie Générale Transatlantique (CGT) took delivery of three similar reefers in 1969/70. The **Pointe Allegre** was followed by the **Pointe Des Colibris** and finally the **Pointe Marin**. All three were built by Cons Nav & Ind de la Mediterranée (CNIM) of La Seyne near Toulon in the south of France, and had a gross tonnage of 6738. The subject of this view, the **Callao**, was previously the **Pointe Des Colibris** and towards the end of the 1970s was sailing for Arcturus Maritime Ltd of Monrovia. She was 481 feet in length and had four holds with six hatches, which were served by six electric cranes of various lifting capacities. She could carry 104 20' containers and had accommodation for five passengers. The **Pointe Des Colibris** had two Pielstick main engines geared to a single propeller shaft driving a controllable-pitch propeller, giving her a speed of 20.5 knots. In 1980 she became the Peruvian flag **Callao** for Naves Frigorificas SA (NAFRISA) and is seen here on the New Waterway on 3 July 1981, looking somewhat the worse for wear. Her final years trading were for Grandluck Maritime Inc, Panama as the **Montego Bay II** from 1982 until 1986. After a period in lay up at Newport, she was sold for demolition at Liverpool in June 1986.

(The late Les Ring)

The **Orque** was one of a series of eight similar ships for eight different French fleets, from the yard of Ateliers et Chantiers de Dunkerque et Bordeaux (France-Gironde) at Dunkerque. She was completed in March 1969 as the **Ivondro** for Havraise and Nantaise and became the **Orque** in 1974 for new owners Compagnie Maritime des Chargeurs Réunis SA (CMCR) of Marseilles. She was a four-hold ship of 8559 grt and with 10153 cubic metres of insulated cargo space. This interesting view of a rather rusty **Orque** was taken from the cliff-top gardens at Penarth Head, late one evening in September 1977. Clearly visible in this photo are her four 5-ton cranes, while in the distance, the freighter **Medcape** (originally **Teakwood** of 1962), is heading down the Bristol Channel. The **Orque** went on to take a further four identities from 1990, which included the name **UB Pride** from 1993 until 1998 for Ugland Reefers Ltd and registered in Nassau, Bahamas. From 1998 she became the **Pride I** for Associated Star Intech Inc Interests of St Vincent and the Grenadines. She was finally sold for breaking up at Mumbai during 1999.

(Bob Allen)

We now pause to study two quite different ships discharging at the East Quay in Newhaven harbour. Newhaven is located on the River Ouse in East Sussex and for many years has been a small but important cross-channel ferry port. Ellerman Lines **Arcadian** makes a fine sight as she is seen discharging in October 1972. She was completed in 1960 by Henry Robb Ltd, of Leith and was an open shelterdeck vessel of 3402 tons gross. She had 835 cubic metres of refrigerated cargo space and her main engine was a 7-cylinder Sulzer of 3500bhp and assembled by Fairfield SB & Eng. Ellerman Lines had a fleet of ships, including the **Arcadian**, that were dedicated to Mediterranean and northern European trade, and did not carry the traditional City names. The **Arcadian** was the last example built to conventional layout for this trade. In 1974 the **Arcadian** was renamed **City of Famagusta** and sold in 1977 to Associated Levant Lines SAL, of Beirut, as **Batroun**. As such she was broken up at Gadani Beach by SZ Enterprises arriving there on 18 December 1986.

(Derek Chaplin)

During the post-war years reefers had regularly called at Newhaven, a practice that eventually ceased in the 1990s. As well as fruit ships, vessels of the Blue Star Line, Royal Mail Lines and Shaw Savill could be found at Newhaven, discharging amongst other commodities, meat from South America. Elders and Fyffes banana boats had been calling at Newhaven for many years, and this view of the 1985-built **Nickerie** dates from 1986. She was completed for Bingo Shipping Co Ltd of Hong Kong and managed by Elders & Fyffes Ship Management. **Nickerie** was built in Japan by Hayashikane Shipbuilding & Engineering Co Ltd of Nagasaki and had a gross tonnage of 4233 and speed of 16 knots. She was 354 feet in length, with three holds and a refrigerated cargo capacity of 5097 cubic metres. Her 7-cylinder engine was a Burmeister & Wain 7L35MC type, built by Hitachi Zosen. She had a near sistership **Jarikaba** which sailed under the Panamanian flag and regularly traded from Portsmouth. By 2008 the **Nickerie** was owned by CV Shipping Co under the Dutch flag and sailing for Seatrade Groningen BV. In 2011 she was thought to be still trading.

(Bernard McCall)

Built between 1968 and 1981, and running to a total of forty ships, the Drammen type pure reefers were without doubt a major success. Eight of these reefers were built in 1972/73 for Maritime Fruit Carriers by Smith's Dock Co Ltd of South Bank on the River Tees. All were given Clipper names, and would appear on the second-hand market from 1976 with the demise of Maritime Fruit Carriers. Cunard Line purchased four of these fast ships and named them **Andania** (ex **Glasgow Clipper**), **Alsatia** (ex **Edinburgh Clipper**), **Andria** (ex **Teesside Clipper**) and **Alaunia** (ex **Cardiff Clipper**). The subject of this view is the Glasgow-registered **Alsatia** of 6680 grt and completed in 1972. She is powered by a 9-cylinder Sulzer diesel built by Clark & NEM Ltd and she had a speed of 23 knots. The **Alsatia** is

seen at Barry on a fine day in July 1977 whilst on charter to Geest. Cunard considered these ships to be attractive purchases at a time when they were keen to get involved in the growing reefer market. However, they were sold after short lives with the company, as they were claimed to be uneconomic to operate. The **Alsatia** departed in 1981 and became the Greek flag **America Freezer**. After further name changes, from 1991 until 1994 she operated for Del Monte Fresh Fruit (International) Ltd as the **Network Swan** and finally **Banana Reefer** from 1993. She was scrapped in Bangladesh in late 1994 by Diamond Steel Products at Bhatiary.

(Bob Allen)

The Drammen design had a very distinctive profile and could be seen throughout the world for well over thirty years. This view clearly shows the distinctive lines of these ships with the foc'sle extended to include No1 hatch. The Panamanian flag **Nordland V** was one of the second series of Drammen reefers often referred to as the Standard Clippers. She was delivered in 1971 as the **Nordland** for Gotaas-Larsen of Norway. She was 6676 grt and had a 9-cylinder Sulzer engine giving her a speed of 22.5 knots. She became the Panamanian-flagged **Nordland V** in 1979 for Reefer Pacific Ganymed Schiffahrtsgesellschaft, which is how we see her on 11 July 1982 on the New Waterway and on charter to Salén. After a spell as the **Arawak** from 1984, in 1985 she reverted to **Nordland V** of Alis Shipping Co SA, Panama. She eventually became the **Arctic Reefer** in 1990, sailing initially under the Cypriot flag and later the Panama flag. As such she foundered on 1 January 1994 in the Pacific Ocean, south-west of Japan, on a voyage from China to Venezuela. Her hull had fractured as a result of earlier collision damage.

(The late Les Ring)

The final quartet of Drammen reefers to be constructed were for Flota Bananera Ecuatoriana SA, the state-owned fruit producer and exporter from Ecuador. They were slightly larger than the earlier Drammen reefers and were generally referred to as Super Clippers. The **Rio Esmeraldas** was completed in August 1979 at Drammen Slip and was followed by the **Rio Chone** in 1980 and **Paquisha** in 1981. A fourth ship was completed in 1980 by Kaldnes at Tonsberg as the **Rio Babahoyo**. The **Rio Esmeraldas** was 6988grt and had a 6-cylinder Sulzer diesel of 11400bhp. She became the **Isla Ferdandina** in 1989 and **Balboa Reefer** in 1995 for Omega Shipping Co Ltd under the Cypriot flag. This is how we see her on 8 October 2000 at Portland Harbour where she was being detained after a problem concerning non-payment of wages to her Russian crew. She sailed for a further eight years taking the name **Kirki** in 2003 and finally **Nordic Cape** in 2004 for Nordic Cape Ltd, flying the St Vincent and the Grenadines flag. She was broken up at Alang in 2008.

(Nigel Jones)

The Drammen reefers often had many name changes during their careers and the **Nordic Ice** was no exception. These vessels were also to be found on charter to many of the big reefer pools such as Salén. **Nordic Ice** is seen arriving at Durban on 6 August 2006 and is flying the flag of St Vincent and the Grenadines. Her owner is given as Bremerton Alliance Ltd, of Kingstown. She began life in 1981 as the **Paquisha** (see caption above), the final Drammen type to be built, and was launched as the **Rio Palora**. She changed name in 1988 to **Isla Isabela** but continued to sail under the Ecuadoran flag. Her dimensions were very similar to **Rio Esmeraldas**, her gross tonnage being 6975, and her cargo handling gear consisted of eight 5-ton derricks. She became the **Orenoco Reefer** in 1995, **Reno** in 1999 and briefly the **Armonia** in 2002 gaining the name **Nordic Ice** later the same year. She too was scrapped at Alang in 2008.

(Trevor Jones)

We now take a look at a few refrigerated ships flying the flags of Communist nations. The Soviet Union was by far the largest operator of refrigerated ships in the world from the 1960s until the late 1980s. However, many of these ships were fish carriers built to act as storage vessels or mother ships for the large Soviet fishing fleets active around the world at this time. The other Communist nations had rather modest fleets of refrigerated ships and Yugoslavia was no exception. The German-built *Marko Polo* was sailing for Mediteranska Plovidba of Dubrovnik when seen here at Cardiff on 18 June 1974. In this view she has been framed by

the bow of a Lauritzen reefer. The *Marko Polo* had been purchased the previous year as the *Crux* from Det Bergenske D/S of Norway. She had, however, started life as the *Cap Domingo* of Hamburg South America Line which disposed of her in 1970. She is a well-kept 17-knot vessel of 3028 tons gross, dating from 1958 and completed by Kieler Howaldstwerke AG Kiel, being similar, albeit slightly smaller, to the ship on page 68. As the *Marko Polo* she was broken up at Split in 1985 by Brodospas.

(John Wiltshire)

Ships of the German Democratic Republic (East Germany) were usually well kept and the reefer **F. Freiligrath** is a good example of this. She is one of a pair of identical ships of 5587 grt obtained by her owner VEB Deutfracht Seerederei of Rostock in 1974. They were built in Scotland in 1967 by Scotts SB & Eng Co Ltd, Greenock for F Laeisz of Hamburg as the **Parma** and **Padua**. The **Parma** became **Parma II** and then **Ferdinand Freiligrath** from 1974, later shortened to **F. Freiligrath** by 1979. The **Padua** became **Georg Weerth** under the East German flag. Each of these fine-looking ships cost approximately £2 million each to build and had accommodation for a crew of fifty . They were classed as open shelterdeck vessels with four holds and eight derricks, and they were powered by a B&W 10-cylinder 2-stroke diesel manufactured by J G Kincaid and giving a service speed of 21 knots. The **F. Freiligrath** was later to become the **Apple Blossom** in 1990 for Elmhurst Shipping Ltd of Panama, and was broken up at Chittagong during 1993. She is seen here on the New Waterway on 22 June 1979.

(The late Les Ring)

In this view we look at a Romanian flag fish carrier receiving attention at Falmouth docks on 7 September 1976. She is named the *Polar IV* and was launched in November 1972 by VEB Mathias-Thesen-Werft, Wismar, in East Germany for the Romanian government fleet Ministerul Industriei Alimentare (Intreprinderea de Pescuit Oceanic) (NAVROM Tulcea) and registered in Tulcea. Completed in 1973, both the *Polar IV* and her sister, *Polar III* of 1972, were 11899 gross tons with a length of 498 feet. As a fish carrier the *Polar IV* would work closely with Romanian trawler fleets acting as a storage vessel for their catch, and as such had four refrigerated holds, with her hull being strengthened to operate in icy waters. Her main engine was a 9-cylinder Halberstadt (MAN) of 9000bhp giving her a speed of 17 knots. The *Polar IV* was broken up in China in 1994, while her sister *Polar III* survived until 2003.

(John Wiltshire)

The **Vasiliy Fesenkov** was a Russian reefer of the B437 type, all of which were built in Poland by Stocznia Gdanska im Lenina of Gdansk. Principal dimensions were either 6399 or 6400 gross tons, with an overall length of 458 feet and a breadth of 59 feet. They were fast ships with a speed in the region of 21 knots, and powered by a Polish-built 2-stroke slow-speed Sulzer diesel engine of 13200bhp. The first of the class was the **Nikolay Kopernik** that was completed in 1974, whilst the last of the series of fourteen built for Russian fleets, was the **Akademik Artobolevskiy** which entered service in 1981. The **Vasiliy Fesenkov** was the fourth B437 built, being new in 1974, and operated for the USSR–Latvian Shipping Co, of Riga. She is seen at Newport on 31 May 1981. In 1991 she became the **Vasilijs Fesenkovs** for Latvian Shipping Company, and was eventually scrapped at Alang during late 1999.

(John Wiltshire)

Another Yugoslav reefer was the **Racisce** of the Mediteranska Plovidba fleet and registered in Dubrovnik. She was a modern yet attractive ship completed in August 1981 by the Brodogradiliste "Split" yard at Split. The **Racisce** was very similar to a trio of Belgian-built reefers from the Boelwerft yard at Tamise, which included the **Pocahontas** of 1980. With a gross tonnage of 7068 she had an insulated cargo space of 12452 cubic metres spread over four holds each with additional access via port and starboard side-access doors in the hull. Her four pedestal-mounted electric cranes were capable of 5-ton lifts. The **Racisce** could also carry 114 20' containers of which 57 could be refrigerated. A fully automated, UMS classed engine room accommodated a 16553bhp, 8-cylinder Tvornica Dizel Motora "Split" slow-speed oil engine to a MAN design giving her a speed of 20 knots. The **Racisce** is seen at Cardiff in her first year, on 16 November 1981, and on charter to Salén. In 1997 she became the **Avocado** for Pisa Shipping Co Ltd of Malta and two years later the **Mahone Bay** under the Antigua and Barbuda flag. Sadly, this fine-looking ship was to arrive at Alang on 2 April 2008 for breaking up carrying the name **Pietari Dream**, having previously sailed for Beetle Transport Inc.

(John Wiltshire)

We now take a look at a wide variety of reefers at work around the world. The reefer *Lucky* is seen here on the move at the French port of Brest on 10 August 1989, with a pilot cutter in attendance. She is on charter to the United Fruit Co, and is carrying the Chiquita brand name on her hull. The *Lucky* is unmistakably one of the former Maritime Fruit Carriers "Core" type reefers, although she is starting to look a little uncared for by her owners Fairway Shipping SA. She was launched on 12 July 1968 as the *Tangerinecore* at the yard of A/S Bergens M/V at Bergen and was 8134 grt. A distinguishing feature of these ships was the two goalpost masts with 10-ton derricks serving No 1 to No3 holds. The large scale disposal of Maritime Fruit Carriers vessels in 1976 witnessed the *Tangerinecore* becoming the *Condata* of Empresa Hondurena de Vapores SA, and later Balboa Shipping Co Inc (both part of the Fyffes Group). In 1988 she became the *Lucky* and was broken up at Alang in 1993.

(Bernard McCall collection)

Looking very much like one of the many attractive reefers built by northern European ship yards with her French-style bipod masts, the **Apple Blossom** is in fact the product of a Japanese shipbuilder. She was completed in 1969 as the **Banagrande** for Bana Shipping Co Ltd of Monrovia and sailed under the Liberian flag. She became the **Apple Blossom** in 1977 for Irvington Investments Ltd, also of Monrovia. She was a product of the Kawasaki Dockyard Co Ltd of Kobe, and had a gross tonnage of 7005 and an overall length of 462 feet. Her main engine was a 9-cylinder MAN of 12600bhp built under licence in Japan. She makes a pleasing sight as she passes inbound along the New Waterway on 24 June 1978. The **Apple Blossom** would eventually meet her end at Chinese shipbreakers in late 1984 after just fifteen years service, a comparatively short life for a reefer.

(John Wiltshire)

In 1971 the first of a new series of 21-knot reefers was introduced to the P&O group of companies. These were intended for operation throughout the world on a variety of trades, and initially they appeared in the house colours of the Federal Steam Navigation Co. The **Wild Auk** was launched on 22 July 1971 having originally been ordered by FM Caribic Frigomaris of Hamburg, but completed for Federal. She was 9603 gross tons, and her builder, A/S Bergens M/V of Bergen had completed her to one of their standard designs with five holds and a refrigerated cargo space of 13634 cubic metres. The **Wild Auk** was followed in 1972 by the **Wild Avocet** and, in 1973 by the **Wild Cormorant** and **Wild Curlew** of 7594 grt, which were completed by a Lübeck shipyard. By the end of 1971 the **Wild Auk** was officially transferred to the P&O General Cargo Division, and is seen here at Cardiff on 14 February 1975. It is pleasing to see that she is still displaying Federal funnel colours, while engaged on the South African fruit run. She was sold to Greek owners in 1980 as the **Olympian Reefer** and then became the **Buenos Aires** in 1989 under Cypriot flag. In 1992 she was sold for service under Panamanian flag, and eventually renamed **Amazon Reefer** by 1995. She was later broken up at Mumbai in 1999.

(John Wiltshire)

Arriving at Barry on the early afternoon tide of 12 February 1995 with a cargo of potatoes is the Cuban flagged reefer **Vinales**. She is a modern and functional-looking ship of 4190 grt with accommodation and engine room aft. Her name is that of a small agricultural town in northern Cuba associated with the production of tobacco and coffee. The **Vinales** was launched on 24 February 1990 by Spanish shipbuilder SA Juliana Constructora Gijonesa of Gijon for Neiviera Castellana SA of Cuba. Her overall length is 345 feet and she has four refrigerated holds of capacity 5728 cubic metres. She can also accommodate forty 20' containers, and has three rather unusual looking 5-ton cranes. The **Vinales** is powered by a 6-cylinder B&W diesel of 4563bhp built by Ast Espanoles SA. Later in 1995, she changed name to become the **Segovia** under Panamanian flag and a year later became the **Aruba** of BV Nautic of the Netherlands. As **Aruba** she spent some time operating in the Seatrade Groningen pool, and in 2011 she is still in service.

(John Wiltshire)

In her original guise as the **Taupo**, the ship in this photograph visited South Wales on a number of occasions together with her three sisters the **Tongariro**, **Tekoa** and **Westmorland**. The **Taupo** was built for the New Zealand Shipping Co Ltd and was launched on 27 August 1965 by Bartram & Sons Ltd of Sunderland. She was the lead vessel in this class with a gross tonnage of 8219 and a speed of 20 knots. These distinctive ships had unusual bipod masts fitted with Hallen derricks to serve their five cargo holds. Most of the cargo space was insulated to take refrigerated goods, and in addition the **Taupo** had four cargo tanks. She passed to associated fleet Federal Steam Navigation in 1969 and by 1973 was part of P&O's General Cargo Division. In 1980 she passed to the Vestey group fleet Austasia Line (Pte) Ltd of Singapore as **Mandama**, a company whose vessels are normally to be found in the southern hemisphere. As the **Mandama** she would trade between New Zealand and the Arabian Gulf with meat, and was therefore an unusual visitor to Newport on 6 May 1982. She was the first of the original quartet to arrive at the breaker's yard, in this case Chittagong, on 29 May 1984.

(Danny Lynch)

Tenerife in the Canary Islands is an important exporter of bananas, even though the fruit is not native to the Island. It is a quality variety of banana, but its small size makes it unsuitable for the main European market, and most consignments go to the Spanish mainland. A variety of reefers like the Japanese-owned **Khalij Reefer** could frequently be seen at the port of Santa Cruz loading bananas. The rugged landscape of this volcanic land mass, makes a fine back-drop, as she prepares to sail on 15 March 1991. Note the pilot ladder is in place, and the funnel markings tell us she is on charter to the Cool Carriers pool. The **Khalij Reefer** was built in 1979 by Kochi Jukogyo KK, Kochi for Asia Reefers KK of Tokyo. She had a gross tonnage of 7701 and an overall length of 461 feet, and the ability to carry road vehicles, in addition to perishable cargo. Power was from a 16-cylinder vee-type Ishikawajima diesel of 13300bhp. Later, in 1991 she changed her name to **Crown Reefer**, becoming **Akaroa** in 1995. Her final guise was as the **Dejima Bay** in 1998 for Akaroa Reefer Inc under the flag of St Vincent and the Grenadines. She was scrapped at Xinhui in China in July 2000.

(Andrew Wiltshire)

The very small reefer **Eskimo** entered service with this name in 1969 for Partrederiet "Eskimo" under Danish flag. Her builder was I/S Ørskovs Staalskibsværft of Frederikshavn who launched her on 16 September 1969 and completed her by December. The **Eskimo** was just 299 gross tons with a length of 187 feet and beam of 33 feet. She had four holds served by a pair of 3-ton derricks, and was powered by an 8-cylinder Alpha-Diesel A/S engine of 800bhp driving a controllable-pitch propeller. In 1981 she became **Fanafrost** for Fanafrost Shipping Ltd under the Gibraltar flag and then reverted to her original name of **Eskimo** in 1988. By now she was sailing for Icelandic Shipping Ltd under the Honduran flag, and this is how we see her in this study. She is believed to be still active in 2011 under the same name, but the owner is now given as Benguela Lines Ltd of Lagos.

(Bernard McCall collection)

Another member of the B437 class of Polish-built reefers (see page 46) was the *Ilya Mechnikov* of 1976. All vessels intended for Soviet fleets were virtually identical and all of them survived the break up of the Soviet Union in 1991. In addition to these the Stocznia Gdanska yard built three similar ships for Empresa Hondurena for service under the Honduran flag. A further three similar ships were built under licence in Spain and Portugal for Polish Ocean Lines and included the *Zyrardow* of 1980. This superb view of the *Ilya Mechnikov* was taken on 25 April 1996 when she was underway in Otago Harbour, New Zealand. By this time she was sailing for the post-Soviet era fleet, Far-Eastern Shipping Co. (FESCO) of Vladivostok. Her gross tonnage was now given as 6412. The *Ilya Mechnikov* became the Panama flag *Komandir* in 2006 for Mechnikov Maritime S.A., and was broken up at Alang, arriving there on 14 May 2008.

(The late Alwyn McMillan - Douglas Cromby collection)

Laid up at Dunkerque on 15 August 1995 are the Greek-flag sisterships **Nissos Limnos** of 1979 and **Nissos Paxi** of 1978. They are typical Japanese-built reefers from the yard of Kochi Jyuko K.K. of Kochi with a gross tonnage of 7577. They were new as the **Freezer Prince** and **Freezer Ace** respectively for Tokumaru Kaiun KK of Tokyo. Features included four side doors to port and starboard, and with the provision for 336 cars if required. Their hulls were 461 feet overall length and the main engine was a 16-cylinder IHI-Pielstick of 13600bhp. The **Freezer Prince** became the **White Billow** in 1983 while the **Freezer Ace** became the **Freezer Leopard** in 1985. After further name changes both vessels eventually took up the identities seen in this view by 1994. The **Nissos Limnos** ended her days trading as the **Spring Reefer** and is thought to have been scrapped in about 2001. The **Nissos Paxi** was broken up at Aliaga in 2005 as the **Blue Reefer**, and registered in Nassau.

(John Wiltshire)

Harsh sunlight bathes the Japanese-built reefer **Atlantic Star** as she is lying at anchor near Piraeus in the summer of 2001. She was completed in December 1983 by Saesbo Heavy Industries Co Ltd at their Sasebo yard, and was the first of two similar ships, the **Pacific Star** following her into service in 1984. The pair were built for Taihei Shipping Co Ltd of Tokyo and had a gross tonnage of 10535. The **Atlantic Star** had an overall length of 497 feet and featured four holds served by five 10-ton electric cranes. Her main engine was an 8-cylinder Mitsubishi of 14400bhp assembled by Ube Industries and giving her a speed of 20 knots. The **Atlantic Star** was very much a typical Japanese-built reefer with distinctive features like aerial masts on her superstructure. By 1992 she was flying the Panamanian flag for T Line Corp SA. Shortly after this view of her was taken, she became the **Atlantic Star** under the Cayman Islands flag for Atlantic Start Shipping Ltd, and in 2003 changed her name to **Stina** for Stina Shipping under the Barbados flag. She was still sailing as such in 2010.

(Peter Fitzpatrick)

The sister to the vessel described on page 33 was the **Polarlicht**, which was completed on 29 September 1964 for Hamburg South America Line (Hamburg-Süd). She was a product of the Blohm and Voss yard at Steinwerder near Hamburg and was very similar in most respects to the **Polarstern**. She had the usual four refrigerated holds, the temperatures of which could be controlled from a console on the ship's bridge. Cargo handling gear consisted of eight derricks and the

Polarlicht was designed to operate with a crew of just twenty-seven. Her main engine was a MAN of 10800bhp and her service speed was 20 knots. She is seen at anchor in 1981 as the **Davao**, and wearing the colours of Fyffes, whose fleet she had joined in 1974. She passed to Hydra Maritime Corp later in 1981 as the **Chion Trader**, and later became the **Banquise** in 1984 under the Greek flag. She was broken up at Gadani Beach in early 1985.

(Bernard McCall collection)

The last ships to be built for the P&O owned British India Steam Navigation Co were a pair of reefers, the **Zaida** and **Zira**. They were completed in 1972 and were intended for use on the Crusader Shipping run, carrying mainly meat between New Zealand and Japan. Both were built by Swan Hunter Shipbuilders Ltd at their Readhead yard in South Shields as refrigerated pallet carriers of 6088 grt. They had two side doors to starboard, and were powered by a 6-cylinder Doxford 67J6C opposed-piston oil engine of 12000bhp. The pair were renamed **Vendee** and **Vosges** respectively in 1975 for continued P&O Steam Navigation service, and were lengthened from 434 feet to 486 feet in 1979/80, giving them a new gross tonnage of around 9204. They were sold as a pair to Ofer Brothers (Ships) Ltd of Israel in 1986 and became the **Avocado Carmel** and **Galia Carmel** registered in Ashdod. The former is seen berthed at Dover's Eastern breakwater on 20 August 1989, where both ships were regular visitors. The **Avocado Carmel** was sold again in 1996 to Ithaca Maritime Corp as the **Carmel Topaz** and managed by Ofer Brothers under the Bahamas flag. Her sister passed to Modet Shipping Corp in a similar arrangement as the **Carmel Exotic**, and both were finally broken up at Alang in 2004.

(John Wiltshire)

The **Blumenthal** was photographed arriving at Durban on a sunny afternoon in November 1969. This may well be the last photograph taken of this ship as, after taking on bunkers in the port, she sailed for the shipbreakers at Kaohsiung, arriving there on 5 December. The **Blumenthal** was the last survivor of the "yacht-like" mail-ships built in the United States in the 1930s. She was launched on 15 August 1931 as the **Segovia** by Newport News SB and DD Co of Newport News, Virginia, and completed in February 1933 as the **Peten** for the United Fruit Company. She was one of six similar ships that also included the **Chiriqui** and **Talamanca**. The **Peten** had a gross tonnage of 6968 and an overall length of 415 feet and speed of 16 knots. She was a twin-screw turbo-electric vessel, and her two General Electric steam turbine/generator sets provided a total of 3360kw power for her propulsion motors. In 1937 she was renamed **Jamaica** for a short charter to Colombian Line, and spent 1942 until 1946 sailing for the US Navy as the **Dione** and later **Ariel**. Reverting to civilian service in 1946 as the **Jamaica**, she continued to sail for United Fruit Mail SS Co Inc of New York with the United Fruit Co as managers, and received a new set of steam turbines in 1950. In 1958 the **Jamaica** was sold to West German owners Union Partenrederei tes. "Blumenthal" (Scipio & Co's) as the **Blumenthal**, where she joined her sistership the **Blexen**, which was the former **Chiriqui**. They were used on services from Bremerhaven to Central and South America and could accommodate forty-eight passengers.

(Trevor Jones)

The **Afric Star** was the first of a class of six 24-knot fully-refrigerated ships for Blue Star Ship Management, and was owned by Glencairn Shipping Co Ltd of London. She was based on a Scandinavian design, and all but one vessel, the **Avila Star** (built in Denmark), were built by Smith's Dock Co Ltd of South Bank on Teesside. The **Afric Star** was completed in February 1975 and her early years were spent operating in the banana trade from Central America to Europe and also the east coast of the United States. She had a gross tonnage of 9784 and five cargo holds, and was fitted with side-doors, five on each side, as clearly visible in the open position in this view. In 1984, the **Afric Star** along with the **Almeda Star**, **Almeria Star** and **Avelona Star** were transferred to a new company Lion Shipping Ltd of Hong Kong, receiving the names **Lanark**, **Harlech**, **Perth** and **Castle Peak** for a short period. Having regained the name **Afric Star** in 1988, she went on to end her days under the Bahamas flag and operating in the Star Reefers pool. She would now be carrying a variety of cargoes ranging from frozen meats to citrus fruit, and was scrapped at Alang in 2001. In this view we see her under repair at Barry on 30 June 1978.

(John Wiltshire)

During 1949 the Government of Argentina took delivery of a quartet of small twin-screw reefers. Two were built at an Italian shipyard in Monfalcone, but the **Rio Quequen** and **Rio Santiago** were constructed on the Isle of Wight by J Samuel White & Co Ltd of Cowes. The latter pair were open shelterdeck vessels of 3263 gross tons with an overall length of 381 feet. They had accommodation for twelve passengers and a crew of forty-eight. A pair of 8-cylinder Burmeister & Wain diesels of 5280bhp total output from Harland & Wolff, gave these ships a speed of 14 knots.

The **Rio Santiago** was launched as **Antartico** for Flota Mercante del Estado, but completed as **Rio Santiago**. In 1961 she was transferred to the Empresa Lineas Maritimas Argentinas fleet. Here we see her passing Rozenburg on the New Waterway on 12 May 1975. Just over a year later the **Rio Santiago** caught fire at Buenos Aires on 13 July 1976 whilst under repair, and was laid up and later offered for sale. She eventually left this port for shipbreakers at Campana on 14 November 1978.

(Paul Boot)

By the 1990s reefers were extremely rare on Merseyside and so the appearance of the **Almarwa** at Liverpool on 26 January 1991 was something of a notable event. She had arrived from her home port of Alexandria with a cargo of potatoes. The **Almarwa** had been built in 1967 by Aalborg Værft A/S as the **Jaslo** for Polish Ocean Lines of Gdynia. As such she was similar to six other vessels built for Poland at this yard, including the **Slupsk** of 1965 and **Sanok** of 1966. The **Jaslo** was a 2309 grt open shelterdeck refrigerated ship with three holds and an overall length of 332 feet, and her hull was strengthened for operation in ice. Her main engine was an 8-cylinder ZUT "Zgoda" (Sulzer) of 3000bhp and she had a speed of 15 knots. She became the **Almarwa** in 1987 for Fahd Navigation & Shipping Co of Alexandria and in 1993 took the name **Noor** for owners in the United Arab Emirates. Her final year of service was 1998, by now named **Zubara**, she caught fire and sank at Port Kuwait on 14 November that year.

(Malcolm Cranfield)

Here we have a modern Chinese-built reefer on charter to Seatrade Groningen. The **Cape Cod** was completed in August 1990 for West German owner DS Rendite Fonds Nr 24 ms "Cape Cod" GmbH. & Co. Kuhlischiff KG, and initially flying the West German flag. At some point between 1993 and this view of her arriving at Newport in October 1994, she took up Liberian registry. The **Cape Cod** was built by the Shanghai Shipyard, as a 6438 grt reefer to ice-class specification, 395 feet in length and 61 feet in the beam. She had four cargo holds served by eight derricks and her masts are seen to be placed high on their deck-houses. This allows the carriage of containers on deck, and her TEU capacity is given as 228. Her main engine is a 5-cylinder Shanghai diesel to a Sulzer design of 9049bhp. This gives her a service speed of 12.5 knots and the **Cape Cod** has the benefit of both bow and stern thruster units. In 2008 she became **Silver Stockholm** under the Norwegian flag, and is thought to be still trading as such in 2011.

(Danny Lynch)

The Bahamas flag **Longva Stream**, seen arriving at Barry on 13 March 1999, was quite an interesting little ship. She was at this time on charter to Seatrade Groningen, and had arrived with a cargo of potatoes. She was one of two identical ro-ro type ships built in 1982 by Astilleros del Atlantico SA of Santander for Corunesa de Navegacion SA, Santander, and they took the names **El Septimo** and **El Octavo**. These ships had a gross tonnage of just 1051 and were 245 feet in length, but with a respectable beam of 47 feet. Their profile was most unusual, and featured a stern door with a ramp. They were not particularly fast ships and each had a 14-cylinder Cons Echevarria diesel of 2100bhp driving a controllable-pitch propeller. Both were converted to reefers in 1987 and the following year the **El Septimo** received a new 12-cylinder Wärtsilä engine of 2990bhp. The **El Septimo** later became the **Frio Baltic** in 1990 and in 1995 took the name **Longva Stream** whilst in port on the River Tyne. She was now owned by Longva Stream Ltd. The last we know of this vessel was that she was sailing as the **Fjord Ice** from 2001 for Fjord Coolers KS of Nassau. She was believed to have become a casualty later that year, and had disappeared from official records by 2004. However, in 2009 she was reported as abandoned at Ancona in Italy.

(Nigel Jones)

The Italian shipyards built very few reefers, but as one might expect, those that were completed were rather distinctive looking ships. Italian shipowner Fratelli d'Amico was operating a fleet of eight purpose-built reefers by 1974, and all were from the builder Ansaldo SpA. The first pair dating from 1963, were named **Mare Italico** and **Mare Somalo**, while the final four were completed in 1966/7. The **Mare Antartico** was one of the 1967 completions at Ansaldo's Muggiano yard near La Spezia. Registered in Palermo, she was 6955 grt and 467 feet in length. She followed the typical reefer layout at this time, with 4 holds, and had accommodation for six passengers. The goalpost masts seem a little out of place but do not spoil her overall appearance. Her fluted funnel carries the colours of Fyffes to whom she must presumably be on charter. The main engine of the **Mare Antartico** was a 9-cylinder Ansaldo Stab Mecc (B&W) diesel of 10800bhp giving her a speed of 20 knots. She is seen underway on the New Waterway on 20 August 1980. Like her sister **Mare Australe**, the **Mare Antartico** was never to receive a change of name throughout her life, and by coincidence, both these vessels were delivered to a shipbreaker at Brindisi on 24 December 1985.

(The late Les Ring)

The *Provincia de el Oro* is a former Scandinavian-built reefer, now flying the flag of Ecuador. She is owned by Naviera del Pacifico SA of Guayaquil and is employed in the banana trade from Ecuador. Here we see her at anchor at Cristobal at the eastern end of the Panama Canal on 10 August 1980. She was completed in 1964 as the *Magleby Mærsk* by Odense Staalskibsværft A/S for AP Møller of Copenhagen, and had a sistership, the *Thurø Mærsk*. The *Magleby Mærsk* had a gross tonnage of 8222 and overall length of 486 feet and speed of 20 knots. Her refrigerated cargo space consisted of four holds incorporating tweendecks to give eight spaces with a total capacity of 9980 cubic metres. Her refrigeration plant manufactured by Stahl allowed perishables to be cooled down to -25°C. Cargo handling gear consisted of eight 5-ton derricks, whilst her main engine which had bridge-control was a 13200bhp 8-cylinder Burmeister and Wain. The *Magleby Mærsk* became the *Pacific Ocean* in 1976 flying the Liberian flag before gaining the impressive name *Provincia de el Oro* in 1979. She was broken up at Alang during 1994 after thirty years trading.

(Andrew Wiltshire)

The Greek flag motor ship *Marietta* is seen arriving at Hull on 9 June 1973. She is owned by Afromar Inc of Piraeus. The *Marietta* started life as the *Port Albany* built in 1965 with a gross tonnage of 8493. She and her sistership *Port Huon* were built by Caledon Shipbuilding and Eng Co Ltd of Dundee for Port Line's Australia to Canada service, and were actually owned by Cunard Line. The *Port Albany* and *Port Huon* proved to be very lively in heavy seas and thus had a poor reputation among the crews. A third similar ship was the *Port Burnie* of 1966, which was built on the Clyde. Nearly all of the *Port Albany*'s cargo space was suitable for refrigerated goods and there were also three tanks suitable for vegetable oils or molasses. They were not designed to carry passengers and the crew would have enjoyed a high standard of accommodation with the benefit of a swimming pool and a hobbies room. An 8-cylinder Wallsend-built Sulzer diesel gave a speed of 19 knots. The *Port Albany* became the *Marietta* in 1972, and a further change of name saw her become the *Artemon* in 1990, for Greek Regular Lines Special Shipping Co Inc, under the Greek flag. She was broken up at Alang during 1992.

(Nigel Jones)

It does seem fitting to include another of the French-built Snow vessels and I have chosen this shot of the **Snow Land** passing Battery Point at Portishead on 16 April 2006. She is now in her twilight years, but still looks to be kept in remarkable condition after thirty-four years service. The **Snow Land** has had many names in her career, the first change being in 1981 when she became the **Malayan King** of Trans-Swedish Shipping Inc flying the Philippine flag, reverting again to **Snow Land** in 1982. Her final three guises were as the **Chiquita Tower** from 1991 until 1994, the **Kyma** from 1994, and finally taking up her original name **Snow Land** in 1997. In this view she was sailing for Neddy Holding SA and wearing the funnel colours of Universal Reefers. These ships had long careers with three members of the class surviving into 2010, but only the **Snow Drift** managed to avoid the breakers that year. The **Snow Land** was sold to Indian shipbreakers and arrived at Alang to be beached on 16 February 2010.

(Nigel Jones)

The **Canterbury Star** was the final member of a class of four identical reefers built for Blue Star Line Ltd by Harland and Wolff Shipbuilding and Heavy Industries Ltd, of Belfast. The lead vessel, **English Star**, was badly damaged by an engine-room fire in the building dock, and consequently was completed after the **Scottish Star** and the **Auckland Star**. All four were designed to operate with a crew of just twenty-one. With a gross tonnage of 10291, the **Canterbury Star** was a modern, attractive reefer following the three-quarters aft layout. She was designed to carry a variety of cargoes such as bananas, citrus fruit and meat. All four holds are fully insulated and accessible through the hatches as well as side doors in the hull. Consideration has been given to palletised stowage and there is provision for 106 containers. Her main engine is a fuel-efficient B&W 7L67GBE type of 15226bhp assembled by her builder and enabling a service speed of 19.5 knots. The **Canterbury Star** is seen at Ghent on 24 July 2008 in the colours of the Star Reefers pool, and at some time previously had been on charter to FII Fyffes Plc. She is clearly in need of some cosmetic attention below the waterline. She arrived at Alang for demolition in June 2011, her name having been changed to simply **Canterbury**.

(Douglas Cromby)

The Fyffes group made a significant investment in new tonnage when they ordered eight new reefers from a Japanese shipyard for delivery from 1969. By this time the existing fleet was somewhat dated with many uneconomical steam-powered ships still in front-line service. The new ships became known as the "M class" and the first ship delivered was the **Matina** in 1969 followed by the **Morant** and **Motagua** in 1970 and **Musa** in 1971. The last vessel of this class was the **Mazatec** in 1973. The **Manistee** was launched on 16 May 1972 by Kawasaki Heavy Industries Ltd of Kobe, and was completed as a 6513 grt ship of overall length 474 feet for Elders and Fyffes Ltd of London. She had a refrigerated cargo capacity of 10709 cubic meters and four 5-ton cranes. Her main engine was a 10-cylinder Kawasaki (MAN design) of 12600bhp coupled to a controllable-pitch propeller. In 1984 the **Manistee** along with three sisterships **Magdalena**, **Manzanares** and **Mazatec** was transferred to Hong Kong-flag, Fyffes-related companies, and **Manistee** became the **Fleet Wave**. She is seen here in Piraeus Roads on 29 September 1990 shortly before becoming the **Mimoza** under the Bahamas flag. She was sold for scrapping at Alang in June 1999.

(Nigel Jones)

A truly beautiful ship, the reefer **Maraki** is seen making her way along the tranquil waters of the Welland Canal in Canada on 13 June 1983. She is setting out on a voyage to Leningrad, with a cargo of frozen poultry from the United States. The **Maraki** was the second of three similar Spanish-built reefers completed by Empresa Nacional "Elcano" of Seville and was launched in December 1961 as the **Northpole**, but not completed until May 1963. The other two ships, the **Tropicana** and the **Southpole** had similar rather drawn out completion periods. The **Northpole** was completed for Liberian Refrigerated Carriers Corp under the Greek flag and had a gross tonnage of 4747. She had a 6-cylinder Sulzer diesel giving her a speed of 18 knots. In 1966 she became the **Atlantic Arrow** for Astroamado Cia Nav SA under the Panamanian flag and from 1967, she took the name **Har Bashan** for "El Yam" Bulk Carriers (1967) Ltd, under the Israeli flag. The year 1973 saw her change to **Assouba** of SITRAM for Ivory Coast owners, and in 1980 she became **Flamingo** for Saronis Shipping Co SA flying the Greek flag. She eventually took the name **Maraki** that we see her carrying in this view in 1983 when she began trading for Sun Coast Maritime Co SA. She was broken up two years later at Gadani Beach.

(Bob Allen)

Cool Carriers was a major operator of reefers and was set up in 1985, to follow in the wake of the Salén business which had collapsed. Cool Carriers operated a large pool of chartered vessels on trading throughout the world. The Philippine flag **Malayan Princess** was a fine-looking ship that dated from 1967. She was 6151 grt and completed by Eriksbergs M/V A/B at Gothenburg for Rederi AB Transatlantic of Sweden, with her registered owner given as Rederiet for ms Tasmanic. She had an overall length of 488 feet and her main machinery consisted of a 7-cylinder Burmeister & Wain engine assembled by the shipyard. In 1978 she became **Regan**, registered in Bristol for Courtwise Ltd and flying the Red Ensign. From 1979 until 1980 she traded as the Liberian flag **Oregano**, and for 1980 only, her name changed to **Coriander** for Atlante Bay Corp. We see her in immaculate condition on the New Waterway on 14 August 1991, and carrying a full set of Cool Carriers branding on her hull, superstructure and funnel. Now named **Malayan Princess** she was flying the Philippine flag for Trans European Shipping Inc, Manila, and managed by Martrade AB. She was broken up at Alang in 1994.

(Rick Garcia - Chris Howell collection)

Clan Robertson of 7955 grt was launched on 3 May 1965 by Greenock Dockyard Co Ltd as the third in a series of four similar ships from the same yard. They were built for Union Castle Mail Steamship Co Ltd and managed by Cayzer Irvine & Co Ltd with all receiving Clan names and livery. These were seasonal fruit ships with some space for meat, and had five holds with tweendecks, providing a total of nineteen cargo spaces, all but one of which were refrigerated. The **Clan Robertson** together with her sisters **Clan Ramsey**, **Clan Ranald** and **Clan Ross** were built at a cost of around £1.95million each and were all regular seasonal visitors to South Wales. Here we see the **Clan Robertson** with her unmistakable funnel, arriving at Cardiff in July 1969 with a cargo of citrus fruit from South Africa. She remained with Union Castle when renamed **Balmoral Castle** in 1976 and later **Balmoral Universal** in 1979. From 1982 she sailed for her final two years as the **Psara Reefer** under the Panamanian flag, arriving at Chittagong in June 1984 for demolition.

(Bob Allen)

The pride of the Maritime Fruit Carriers fleet were the four ships often referred to as the "Queencores" of 1972/73. Named **Gladiola**, **Orchidea**, **Iris Queen** and **Chrysantema** they were all built by Aalborg Værft A/S in Denmark. When Maritime Fruit Carriers ceased to trade, the Cunard Steamship Company quickly purchased all four ships and renamed them **Saxonia**, **Servia**, **Scythia** and **Samaria** respectively. At 575 feet in length and 12182 tons gross, they were large modern reefers and at the time must have been a good purchase. In this view taken at Birkenhead on 27 September 1985 we see a group of Cunard reefers laid up. Prominent are the **Servia** and **Scythia**. The **Servia** was sold the same year and became Greek flag **Castor** changing to **Kastora** in 1988. She caught fire in 1989, and was scrapped at Gadani Beach in 1990 as the **Marwan IX**. The **Scythia** became the Greek flag **Centaurus** for Toulon Shipping Corp in 1986, and by coincidence caught fire in the United States in February 1989. She was broken up at Chittagong shortly after. These five-hold ships had a speed of 24 knots.

(John Wiltshire)

The Cypriot flag **Northern Ice** was yet another splendid example of a West German-built reefer that had spent her early years trading for Hamburg-Süd. She was built by Kieler Howaldtswerke AG at Kiel as the **Cap Valiente** and was launched on 29 September 1959. She entered service in 1960 as the second ship of a pair, the **Cap Corrientes** being the first. At 4113 gross tons she was a closed shelterdeck ship ship capable of accommodating five passengers. Her refrigerated capacity was 6607 cubic metres and her main engine, a 9-cylinder MAN assembled by the shipyard gave her a speed of 17.5 knots. In 1970 she became the **Cacique Yanquetruz** under the Argentinian flag, and in 1972 the **Northern Ice** for Libramar Shipping Co Ltd of Famagusta, and this is how we see her in 1973. In 1982 she was still trading, but as the Greek-owned **Falcon** and ended up at Gadani Beach for scrapping in 1984.

(John Wiltshire collection)

The **Dole Africa** was one of a class of four similar modern refrigerated container and pallet carriers built for Dole Fresh Fruit International of Nassau and flying the Bahamas flag. All were delivered in 1994 with the **Dole Africa** being the last in the series completed in December. She was built in Poland by Stocznia Gdanska SA of Gdansk and had a gross tonnage of 10584. She had an overall length of 494 feet and a beam of 74 feet. The palletised cargoes were carried in four refrigerated holds with a total of 14838 cubic metres capacity. These four ships could carry 264 containers and the cargo handling gear consisted of a pair of 32-ton and a pair of 8-ton cranes. The **Dole Africa** was a 22-knot ship powered by a 6-cylinder B&W diesel of 15515bhp built by Hyundai Heavy Industries. She is seen here at Walsoorden on 28 May 2002. Her sisterships were the **Dole America**, **Dole Asia** and **Dole Europa**. All four reefers were still trading under their original names in 2010.

(Douglas Cromby)

Belgian flag reefers were few and far between, but shipowner Belgian Fruit Lines SA of Antwerp had a fleet of six very smart vessels dating from 1965 to 1967. All were built by J Boel et Fils SA (Boelwerf), at Tamise in Belgium and the *Frubel Prinses Paola* was the final ship delivered in 1967. She had a gross tonnage of 5154 and a service speed of 21 knots. Her main engine was an 8-cylinder MAN diesel of 10680bhp, assembled by ACEC. She was a rare visitor to South Wales and is seen sailing from Cardiff on a rather gloomy 12 June 1975, after discharging oranges from Israel. The *Frubel Prinses Paola* is an attractive ship, spoilt only by her work-stained hull. She was sold in 1978 to Intercontinental Transportation Services Ltd of Monrovia and took the new name *Santa Marta*. In 1982, her final guise was as the *Coentroeverett* under the Philippine flag. She continued to trade for a further ten years, and was not broken up until July 1992 when she arrived in China.

(John Wiltshiire)

The *Del Monte Planter* was built in 1989 for Harley Shipping Corp of Monrovia for service under the Liberian flag. She was a modern Spanish-built reefer of 8945 grt, the first in a series of four, the others being the *Del Monte Harvester*, *Del Monte Packer* and *Del Monte Transporter*. The same yard, Astilleros Espanoles SA (AESA) of Sevilla also delivered a larger pair of reefers in 1991. The *Del Monte Planter* was designed for palletised cargoes and could take 248 20' containers. She had four holds of total capacity 10706 cubic metres served by four 19-ton electric-cranes. Her main engine was a 6-cylinder B&W of 11924bhp, assembled by the shipyard giving her a speed of 20 knots. In 2000 she had her name shortened to simply *Planter*, and now owned by Neutron Ltd, she remained under the Liberian flag. We see her as *Del Monte Planter* underway off Terneuzen in April 1998 and clearly showing her Del Monte branding.

(Douglas Cromby)

In 1983 J Lauritzen took the first of eight large reefers from shipyards in the Far East. The first ships were the **Anne B.** and **Betty B.**, built in Japan for Norwegian owners and charter to the Lauritzen pool. The next four ships came from South Korean builder Hyundai Heavy Industries Co Ltd, of Ulsan and included the **American Reefer** of 1985, while the final pair new in 1988, were once again from Japan and included the **Argentinean Reefer**. The **Anne B.** and **Betty B.** became the **Belgian Reefer** and **Brazilian Reefer**, respectively, in 1992. Both had been built by Hashihama Zosen of Tadotsu as 12383 grt ships featuring four holds with fifteen tweendeck spaces, and the ability to take 152 containers (76 refrigerated) as well as vehicles. Power was from a 6-cylinder IHI-Sulzer-6RTA58 engine of 9450bhp, giving them a speed of 18 knots. The **Belgian Reefer** was to work in the Lauritzen Cool pool from 2000 when J Lauritzen took over Cool Carriers from Hoegh of Norway. From 2007 Lauritzen ceased to operate reefers and Lauritzen Cool became NYKCool. The **Belgian Reefer** makes an impressive sight as she passes Calshot on 5 April 2009. She is now owned by Prow Shipping of the Bahamas, and does not really show any obvious signs of her twenty-six years active service.

(Douglas Cromby)

Fruit juice carriers are few in number, and although in more recent years some have been purpose built as such, this example is a conversion. The **Citrus do Brasil** was built in 1970 as the **Navelinacore** for Maritime Fruit Carriers. After her sale and several name changes, she was converted from a reefer into a fruit juice carrier in 1982 and renamed the **Ouro do Brasil** under the Liberian flag. Her sistership **Sultana** became the fruit juice carrier **Sol do Brasil** in 1984. As **Navelinacore** she had been built in Norway by A/S Bergens M/V of Bergen and had a 7-cylinder Akers/Nylands Verksted (B&W) diesel of 11500bhp. After conversion she retained just one hold, but in addition now had seven special tanks of 7932 tonnes total capacity, and discharge was achieved with seven cargo pumps. In 1992 the **Ouro do Brasil** became the **Citrus do Brasil** of MV Pasadena Shipping Corp, Monrovia, still under the Liberian flag. She is seen at Cardiff on 13 April 1998 where she was being used as a storage vessel for concentrated fruit juice, brought in by more modern tankers like the 1994-built **Sol do Brasil**. The **Citrus do Brasil** was broken up in India during 2003.

(Nigel Jones)

As briefly mentioned earlier, fish carriers at one time represented quite a high proportion of the world's refrigerated ships. Therefore, we shall take a look at a few more of these specialist vessels. In 1975 the Russians purchased the modern "fast" reefers **Brunstor** and **Brunshoeft** from W Bruns of Hamburg. The latter became the **Dnestrovskiy Liman** and is the subject of this view taken on 1 March 1978 at Las Palmas in the Canaries. Both vessels were converted for use as fish carriers and were thus officially re-classified as such. The **Dnestrovskiy Liman** became part of the USSR-Mortransflot fleet registered in Kaliningrad and being of ice-class construction, was suitable for deployment in many areas in support of the fishing fleets. As a reefer she had been built in 1966 by Rheinstahl Nordseewerke of Emden and had a gross tonnage of 4639 grt. Her main engine was an 8-cylinder MAN of 9600bhp and her service speed was 21 knots. The **Dnestrovskiy Liman** was to be broken up at Alang in 1994. Her sister the **Dneprovskiy Liman** (ex **Brunstor**) met her fate at Alang in 1996.

(John Wiltshire collection)

Some non-communist yards completed a number of fish carriers for the Soviet fleets, and one such vessel was the **Ostrov Atlasova** of 1971. She had been launched by Lindholmens Varv A/B, Gothenburg, on 16 September 1970 as a 9737 grt, 493 foot long ship with six cargo holds. She was one of a class of twelve similar ships from this yard, that commenced with the **Ostrov Russkiy** in 1969. By 1992 the **Ostrov Atlasova** was part of the USSR "Zapryba" fleet based upon Kaliningrad in the Baltic. She was a single-screw vessel, but with two Pielstick-type main engines of 12000bhp total. She changed names several times from 1992 becoming the **Atlasova Sala**, then **Lord Lady** in 1998 and **Aqua Frost** in 1999. Her final name was **Win Far No.101** under the Panamanian flag, but with no recorded owner. She was broken up some time in 2005, possibly in China. This view of her as **Win Far No. 101** was taken on 26 March 2001 at Ko Sichang, south of Bangkok. She was receiving some repair work whilst at anchor.

(Nigel Jones)

The Polish-built **Roztocze** was the sixth member of a class of eight fish carriers known as the B364 series. All were built by Stocznia Gdanska im "Lenina" of Gdansk commencing in 1986 with the **Kociewie** of 8833 grt, and ending with the Cypriot flag **Chiquita Abava** of 7057 grt in 1992. The **Roztocze** was completed in March 1991 for Transocean Shipping Co Ltd of Cyprus and had a gross tonnage of 7389. She was built as a refrigerated fish carrier and her hull was strengthened for operation in ice. As can be seen in this view, she has a substantial amount of accommodation, given her overall length of just 407 feet. This would no doubt be explained by her additional role when built as a support ship for trawling fleets. She is just one month old when photographed on the New Waterway in April 1991, and her colour scheme softens her somewhat severe lines. The **Roztocze** features goalpost masts with eight derricks and can also carry eight 20' size containers. Her main engine is a 6-cylinder H Cegielski (B&W) of 6118bhp giving her a speed of 18 knots. After a decade she became **Marianao Ice** for Arkis Star Shipping Co Ltd, of Limassol, and continued to fly the Cypriot flag. She is thought to be still in service in 2011.

(Douglas Cromby)

Any shipowner will know only too well what happens when you bring steel into contact with salt water. Thankfully most ships are well kept, protected with regular fresh coats of paint. Sadly, the subject of this view is a victim of neglect, to put it mildly. However, combined with the late evening sun, all this rust makes for a dramatic image. The Cypriot flag *Zolotaya Dolina* was new in 1986, and was the second of eight similar ships, built by G P Sudostroitelnyy Zavod IM "61 Kommunara" of Nikolayev. This series was completed between the years 1985 and 1988, the final example being the **Anton Gurin**. These were built as fish carriers and the *Zolotaya Dolina* was to enter service for Ussuri Shipping Co and registered in Vladivostok under the Russian flag. She had a gross tonnage of 6648 and her hull was naturally strengthened for operation in ice. She had four cargo holds served by 8 derricks and a service speed of 15 knots. She is seen sailing from Barry on 29 June 1999 bound for Falmouth and lay-up. The *Zolotaya Dolina* had arrived at Barry from Cyprus with a cargo of potatoes. Later that year she became **Soraksan** for Neutrinos SA flying the Panamanian flag. In 2010 she was still trading as **Soraksan** with Panamanian registry but owned by Vostoktransshipping Co Ltd of Russia.

(Nigel Jones)

Since the late 1960s, the elimination of refrigerated cargo liners and the gradual decline in the numbers of refrigerated ships and pure reefers at work on our oceans has been the result of the increasing global containerisation of shipping. Container ships often have facilities to accommodate a reasonable number of refrigerated units. These containers are either plumbed into the ship's own specialist system or run their own refrigeration plant. An early container ship with a small amount of integral refrigeration capability was the Japanese *Hikawa Maru* of 1974. She was typical of many large container ships at this time, being 700 feet in length and 24770 grt. Her TEU capacity was 1277 of which 157 places were available to refrigerated containers. She was built by Nippon Kokan KK at their Tsurumi Shipyard in Yokohama for shipowner Nippon Yusen Kaisha & Showa Kaiun KK, Tokyo. The *Hikawa Maru* was a fast vessel and 23 knots was achievable thanks to a large 9-cylinder IHI Sulzer of 36000bhp. This dramatic view of the *Hikawa Maru* was taken in June 1987 from the Lion's Gate Bridge at North Vancouver, a fine structure dating from 1938. The following year she became the *Hikawa II* for Aquarius Shipholding SA under Liberian registry, and was scrapped at Chittagong in 1998.

(Rick Garcia - John Wiltshire collection)

The Shipping Corporation of New Zealand Ltd was established as a shipping company in 1973 by the New Zealand government and continued as such until 1989. Only a handful of ships were operated, the largest of which was the **New Zealand Pacific**. She was a container vessel of 43704 grt completed in 1978 by Bremer Vulkan AG and registered in Wellington, probably the largest ship ever registered in that port. She was a massive 815 feet overall length and 106 feet in the beam. The **New Zealand Pacific** was a twin-screw ship with a pair of 8-cylinder MAN engines of 53820bhp giving her a speed of 23 knots. Her total TEU capacity was 1822 of which 1223 could be refrigerated. She is seen here on the New Waterway on 3 April 1983, and unusually her decks appear to be devoid of containers. The **New Zealand Pacific** carried the name **Tui** for a brief period in 1989 before reverting to her original name for the remainder of her trading days. By 1996 she was sailing for P&O Containers Ltd under the Hong Kong flag and by 2000 she was recorded as being owned by P&O Nedlloyd Ltd and registered in Bermuda. The **New Zealand Pacific** was broken up at Jiangyin in 2002.

(John Wiltshire collection)

On 1 January 1978, Bank and Savill Line was formed to provide a joint container service between the US Gulf and Caribbean via the Panama Canal to Australia and New Zealand. Trading commenced using chartered tonnage. In 1980, now joined by the Shipping Corporation of New Zealand, three new purpose-built refrigerated container ships were placed on the run, the **Dunedin**, seen here in 1983 at Auckland, being the contribution by Shaw Savill, and also that company's first cellular container ship. She was completed by Swan Hunter Shipbuilders Ltd at the Walker shipyard on Tyneside as a 768 TEU container ship. She had seven holds, and of these, No 1 and No 7 could also take break-bulk or palletised cargo. Of 18140grt, the **Dunedin** was powered by a 6-cylinder Harland & Wolff (B&W) engine of 20500bhp giving her a speed of 19 knots. In 1986 she was sold to West German owner Hamburg-Südamerikanische as the **Monte Pascoal**, and an additional cargo section was added by Flender Werft of Lübeck. This increased her length from 578 to 663 feet, and her overall beam from 88 feet to 98 feet; her TEU capacity rose to 1114. Between 1990 and 2001 she had many changes of name, and her final years were as the Panamanian flagged **MSC Jessica**. She was broken up in India at Alang in 2009.

(Don Meeham - Chris Howell collection)

The Singapore-owned *Sea Elegance* is seen at anchor off Singapore on 18 July 1999. She had carried a number of names but entered service in 1980 as the *Willowbank* for Bank Line (Andrew Weir & Co Ltd). In this view she is owned by Pacific International Lines (Pte) Ltd, and had previously been the *California Star* from 1989 to 1996, and prior to that, Australasia Line's *Mandowi* after sale by Bank Line in 1988. As built she had a gross tonnage of 18236, but by the time of this photograph it was recorded as 17789. She was completed in June 1980 by Smith's Dock Co Ltd of South Bank on Teesside as a part-refrigerated container ship and general cargo ship. She had seven holds and could accommodate 768 TEU containers of which 368 could be refrigerated. Cargo handling was by way of four Hagglund 36-ton electric cranes. Her main engine was a 6-cylinder J G Kincaid (B&W) of 20460bhp installed in a fully-automated engine room. She was to be the last new ship built for Bank Line and also the only purpose-built container ship ever owned by them. In October 2003 as the *Sea Elegance* she suffered a serious accommodation fire and was sold. Later repaired, she re-entered service as the *Golden Gate* for Four Seasons Maritime SA sailing under the Panamanian flag. By this time she had lost her four cranes. She was sold in early 2009 by South Korean owners Sinokor Merchant Maritime Co Ltd to breakers at Alang.

(Douglas Cromby)

This impressive shot of the Greek-owned *Cap Vilano* underway in the Elbe Estuary was taken on 28 May 1997. She was a part-refrigerated container ship, built some twenty years earlier in Poland by Stocznia Gdanska at Gdansk. She was launched in April 1977 as the *Adviser* for Charente SS Co Ltd, with T & J Harrison as managers, and followed her near sister *Astronomer* into service. She had a gross tonnage of 27754, and four holds, each made up of six individual compartments. She could carry 1416 20' containers of which 302 could be refrigerated, and a notable feature was her ability to handle her own cargo by means of a Liebherr 40-ton gantry crane. Her main engine was a 10-cylinder H Cegielski (Sulzer) of 29000bhp and she also featured a bow-thruster unit. In 1983 she went on charter to Seawinds of Hong Kong as *Asia Winds*, before another charter in 1985 to CGM as *CGM Provence*, by which time her TEU capacity had increased to 1520. In 1990 she reverted to *Adviser* as one of the last two Harrsion ships left in service, and in 1993 was sold to Toddle Shipping Inc, Liberia (Costamare Shipping Co) under the Greek flag and immediately chartered to Laser Line of Sweden as *Laser Stream*. A further charter from Costamare Shipping saw her become *Cap Vilano* in 1996, and then *MSC Namibia* in 2001, operated by the Mediterranean Shipping Company. In 2010 she was still sailing as *MSC Namibia* but she passed to Indian shipbreakers at Alang in April 2011.

(John Wiltshire)

Another part-refrigerated fully-cellular container ship was the **Safmarine Cotonou** of 1986, a ship which carried several names in her twenty-three year career. She was launched on 21 September 1985 by Flender Werft AG at Lübeck for K Ivarans Rederi GmbH & Co under the West German flag, and with the name **Santa Catarina**. Completed in 1986, she was 587 feet in length with a gross tonnage of 21054. She had a 1737 TEU container capacity including 100 refrigerated units and she was fitted with four cranes. The **Santa Catarina** was an 18-knot ship powered by a 7-cylinder 2-stroke B&W oil engine of 16559bhp. Name changes started in her first year when she became **Scandutch Edo**, becoming **Nedlloyd Van Linschoten**

in 1989 **Zim Australia** in 1994. The nature of the container shipping business meant that charters were the norm, and inevitably a name change took place to reflect this. She sailed with the name **Maersk Cotonou** from 1998 until 2000, when still under Mærsk Group ownership, she became the **Safmarine Cotonou** for The Mærsk Co Ltd (Safmarine Ship Management). She was now registered in Douglas and flying the Isle of Man flag, and this is how we see her on the River Seine at Rouen on 5 April 2003. She was broken up in China at Jiangyin, arriving there in late 2009.

(John Wiltshire)